OBSERVING BRITISH AND EUROPEAN MAMMALS

CHRISTIAN BOUCHARDY
FRANÇOIS MOUTOU

OBSERVING BRITISH AND EUROPEAN MAMMALS

TRANSLATED BY
IAIN BISHOP

BRITISH MUSEUM (NATURAL HISTORY)

British Library Cataloguing in Publication Data

Bouchardy, Christian
  Observing British and European mammals
1. Europe. Mammals — Field guides
I. Title II. Moutou, François
III. Observer les mammiferes sauvages.
English

599.094

ISBN 0–565–01095–6

A volume created by A.T.P. with the collaboration of:
Michele Clouvel, Evelyne Cornille, Thierry Descamps,
Pierre Enjelvin, Noel Gouilloux, Jean–Bernard Rioual

© English translation British Museum (Natural History) 1989
First published in 1989
British Museum (Natural History)
Cromwell Road
London SW7 5BD

Printed in Spain by Graficas Estella SA

CONTENTS

ABBREVIATIONS

These are found only on the table of footprints
(Pages 38–44)
AD fore right.
PD hind right.

PHOTOGRAPH ACKNOWLEDGEMENTS

The photographs in this book were provided by NATURE Agency,
B.P. 75. 63405 Chamalieres Cedex, France.

BIGNON: 120; BOUCHARDY: 17R, 17L, 29T, 36, 45, 49, 52, 61,
64L, 64R, 65L, 65R, 129, 132T, 132B, 133, 136T, 140, 141, 153, 159,
184T, 184B, 200, 204T, 204L, 204R, 208T, 208B, 213B, 220B,
225, 229T; CHAUMETON/CHOUSSY: 128; CHAUMETON/
LANCEAU: 72, 145, 181; DALTON/NHPA: 8, 77, 88, 89, 100;
DURANTEL: 17R, 28, 41, 53, 125, 136B, 189, 201, 212, 217B, 221;
ENJELVIN: 217T, 229B; FERRERO: 21, 116, 137; FIDLER/
OKAPIA: 188; GOHIER: 157; LANCEAU: 13, 84, 112, 149T, 164,
168, 220T: LEACH/NHPA: 108; MOUTOU: 37, 124; NATURE: 12,
68, 158, 177; REINHARD/OKAPIA: 156, 165, 193, 205, 213T;
SAUER: 29B, 176, 197; SAUNIER: 24, 172; SCHREMPP/OKAPIA:
173; SIEGEL: 20, 25, 149B, 228.

DISTRIBUTION MAPS

Distribution maps have been included for some species to supplement the distribution data in the text. These maps have been
carefully prepared to summarise up–to–date knowledge.
However, the distribution limits of several mammals are poorly
known for a variety of reasons. Some species have been little
studied, others have been considerably reduced in numbers and
some populations have completely disappeared, whilst other
species have been introduced and some species are extending
their range. As a result the data changes rapidly and the maps in
this work can only provide a momentary static image of the real
situation as it appears in the nineteen–eighties in western
Europe. Changes which can be detected are indicated in the
text.

It must be remembered that a species will only occur in certain types of habitat within its geographical range and it is the
microhabitat conditions that determine the presence or absence
of a species at the local level.

PREFACE

Finding and observing mammals cannot be successfully achieved by chance. To obtain meaningful results three conditions must be fulfilled. The student must be able:

* to know how to recognise indications of presence
* to recognise the species quickly
* to know their behaviour patterns and the places where they live.

The aim of this book is to help the reader to satisfy these conditions.

The discovery of an indication (track, dropping etc.) can put the observer on the right lines but little benefit accrues if he cannot then place it in context. To go beyond the collection of footprints and incidental observation it is essential to know why an animal lives in a given place and the manner in which it organises its life in its vital range.

This is why this book describes, species by species, the essential knowledge about the ways of mammals, after having summarised in the first part the many indications which they leave in the field.

The task of the amateur mammal watcher can be eased by learning to search for animals in various ways: through indications, habitat or by observing the animal itself.

Good tracking and good watching.
The authors.

MAMMALS INCLUDED IN THIS GUIDE

Of the 4000 species of mammals known in the world, only a fraction, about 200 species, are found in western Europe. This figure includes the marine mammals around our shores which are not included in this book.

The Class is divided into Orders the names of which reflect various aspects of their lifestyles or structure: feeding habits (insectivores, carnivores), method of locomotion (ungulates, chiroptera), dentition (rodents).

INSECTIVORES

This group contains an assemblage of small mammals that are morphologically very different from each other, for example moles, shrews and hedgehogs. It is thought that some of the insectivores have traits in common with some of the earliest known mammal species. This does not mean, however, that the living representatives of this group are primitive but it is probable that their characteristics appeared very early. If they have been conserved it is because the corresponding adaptations have proved useful.

The insectivores include the small terrestrial and burrowing hunters of invertebrates (i.e. insects in particular), armed with numerous pointed teeth. In the hedgehogs and the shrews the first incisors are crotchet shaped and well developed. In contrast the moles have a more 'classical' dentition with fang–like canines.

The species of insectivores living in Europe have five digits on each foot. Whilst the hedgehog sleeps all winter and the mole makes provision for winter feeding, the shrews, because of their very small size and year round activity, are subject to many ecological and physiological problems of astonishing magnitude, for example overcoming the rigours of winter and resisting the predation of carnivores. The bitter taste of their flesh repels most terrestrial carnivores and only the predatory birds consume them in any numbers – the remains of shrews are often found in the reject pellets of raptors.

RODENTS

Almost half the known species of mammals are rodents. They are an adaptable group particularly able to colonise a large variety of habitats, from the marmot of the Alps and the red squirrel of the

The stoat, a carnivore, seen here in its summer coat.

forests, to the terrestrial, subterranean and aquatic voles. All possess two pairs of continuously growing incisors (one above and one below) which are separated from the cheek teeth by the very characteristic diastema, a space without teeth.

Within this group a variety of feeding habits are found. Although all rodents are essentially plant–eaters, feeding on herbs, trees, fruit, grain, roots, etc. small amounts of meat may supplement the vegetable diet. The brown rat is almost omnivorous which helps to explain its adaptability.

The rodents are renowned for their proliferation, especially the voles, rats and house mice. Other species such as the marmot and the beaver have much slower reproductive cycles adapted for a different pattern of life.

Rodents are everpresent in our everyday lives: certain species live close to man while others colonise cultivated areas. This is why the peaks of population (plagues) sometimes observed are so important especially in the case of certain voles.

The small species of rodents are the staple diet for numerous carnivores (mammals, birds and snakes).

Lagomorphs

The hares and rabbits form a group separate from the rodents although from the morphological and behavioural point of view there are many similarities. There is, however, one anatomical character that distinguishes them – they possess two small additional incisor teeth behind the upper pair. The general morphology of the species present in Europe (terrestrial, hopping animals with long ears) permits instant recognition.

The lagomorphs have an unusual process of digestion in that it involves refection: the animal reingests soft pellets produced during the day, passing food a second time through the digestive system before producing the characteristic hard fibrous droppings.

Ungulates

There are two principal orders in the ungulates: the perissodactyls, including horses, in which the axis of symmetry of the foot passes through the third digit, and the artiodactyls in which the axis of symmetry passes between the third and fourth digits. The wild European species are all artiodactyls, belonging to the suids (pigs), cervids (deer), or bovids (goat, chamois, ibex).

The wild boar, ancestor of our domestic pig, is the only non–ruminant ungulate and it is also the only omnivorous species.

Cervids and bovids are strictly herbivorous. Rumination allows them to assimilate substances such as cellulose, thanks to the work of the microflora and fauna of the complex stomach – a veritable biological factory.

The dentition of the wild boar is complete. The two sexes, particularly the males, develop tusks – large canine teeth, the upper ones curving upwards inside the lower straight pair.

The ruminants (cervids and bovids) do not have upper incisors and have a diastema between the lower incisors and the cheek teeth (premolars and molars).

Amongst the cervids only the males possess antlers which are lost and replaced each year. In the bovids, on the other hand, both the males and females have horns, which consist of a hollow horn case, overlying a bony core. The horns of these animals grow continually throughout their lives.

Local extinctions, reintroductions and translocations have considerably modified the distribution and composition of the wild populations of ungulates especially amongst the mountain species (e.g. chamois, ibex and mouflon).

CARNIVORES

The terrestrial carnivores are sometimes called fissipedes (in contrast to the marine carnivores – pinnipedes – which are not dealt with here). This group comprises mammals of a wide range of sizes and weights, for example, the female weasel may weigh a mere 50 g whereas a brown bear of the Pyrenees or the Abruzzes may reach 200–300 kg.

The dentition of carnivores is characteristic: it comprises well developed canines (the fangs) and two special cheek teeth (the carnassials). These are the very sharp fourth upper premolar and the first lower molar which are used for shearing flesh. Within this group there is a variety of dietary regimes. The strictest carnivores are, on the one hand the felids (e.g. wild cat and lynx) and on the other hand the small mustelids (e.g. weasels and stoats). The marten is a voluntary frugivore (i.e. fruit and seed eater) as is the badger. The fox regularly consumes green plants, and the otter fish. The bear is omnivorous, its food consists largely of vegetation. As carnivores are always at the top of the food chain they are extremely sensitive to any disruption of the environment. The populations of certain species are very low (e.g. bear, otter and lynx), and near to critical levels in Europe. The bear has almost totally disappeared from mainland Europe and completely from the British Isles. These regressions or disappearances are caused by hunting or by massive modifications of

The rabbit, a lagomorph.

the habitats with especially severe consequences for those species that need large areas to survive. Man is one of the principal predators and does not always show sufficient tolerance of his competitors, notably when he seeks to protect his domestic livestock and game.

CHIROPTERA

There are about 30 species of bats found in Europe. The order includes a quarter of all the known species of mammals and they are an important but poorly understood group. Of all the mammals only the bat is capable of flying. All the European species are insectivorous and this forces them to hibernate during the winter when their prey becomes scarce and hard to find. Their biology is marked by phases of activity followed by periods of rest (night/day, summer/winter). It seems that the numerous phases of rest are correlated with the astonishing longevity of some species – up to 30 years in the rhinolophs.

In contrast the life expectancy of a vole, which is of a similar weight, is only 18 months.

The bats use a sonar system – that is a system of sound echoes sent and received, which enables them to navigate in the dark and chase their prey. The emissions are in the ultrasonic range but some human ears are capable of hearing some of the frequencies used in nocturnal flight. Each species has its own sound 'identity card' apparatus capable of decoding the emissions to the audible range can be used to identify the species.

Many bats are linked to human habitats (roofs and mines) which they may frequent in summer, in winter or even all the year round. They are extremely vulnerable to the massive use of insecticides in agriculture and in domestic pest control and to the disastrous ringing campaigns of the 1960s.

The red squirrel, a likeable rodent.

Domestic animals

Cattle, sheep, goats, pigs, horses, cats and dogs belong to a variety of mammal groups and each is derived from wild species now mostly disappeared. The fact that they live in the domestic state signifies essentially that, contrary to wild animals, they are raised and protected by man. They are widely distributed and are found in all zones inhabited by humans. It is probably their tracks and signs that one encounters most often. Also it is usual to think of the dog before thinking of the wolf, of the domestic cat before thinking of the wild cat and of the goat before thinking of the roe deer. It is important to know how to recognise their signs in order to identify more easily the remains of the wild species.

Introduction to the Ecology of Mammals

Role and behaviour of mammals in their habitats

As most of the observations of mammals or their traces take place in the field it is important to know something of their ecology. This enables us to explain and predict the presence of a species and its traces, thereby making fieldwork trips more fruitful and interesting.

Relationships between animal species

When facing questions about animal ecology it is always necessary to remember that the distribution of species and the relationships between them are not just the product of chance. Walking in woodland, on grassland or in the mountains animal signs or even the animal itself may be observed and if careful note is taken of the season, the hour of the day, the type of countryside together with the name of the species seen it becomes noticeable that associations are repeated. This is true not only for mammals but also for most animal species. If observation is sufficiently systematic it can shed light on some of these associations (between species; species and habitat, etc.) and to the subtle differences in apparently homogeneous assemblages such as a forest or cultivated plain. For this reason it is preferable to visit a single location regularly to get to know its characteristics well, before testing your sense of observation on unknown habitats.

Food chains

The presence of a species in a habitat is directly linked to the food resources which it finds there. The most numerous mammals are the herbivores (rodents, lagomorphs, ungulates) in temperate regions. They feed on plants and transform vegetable protein into animal protein. At each transformation there is a loss of energy and a food chain linking plants to carnivores, passing through the herbivores, passes through the most common animals to the most rare.

In a natural habitat, the food chain forms a complex network because the component species are often opportunistic, capturing the most easily available prey. For example, the otter which is habitually a fish eater may occasionally eat rodents, as does the stoat, or frogs, equally mink and weasel may be the victim of a wild cat. The diet of each species may be more or less narrow. In some 'simple' habitats, notably on islands, there are often fewer species than on continental areas. Also animals on islands consume a greater variety of prey species than on continental masses. Their morphology may also evolve as a consequence (see lesser white–toothed shrew and Corsican weasel).

Predator–prey relations

The line or lines linking predators and prey are an often discussed aspect of ecology. The problem may be simply posed as follows: why is it that more roe deer are found in areas where there are lynx that

The genet's toilet.

prey on them? The answer is not a simple one because it involves understanding phenomena which have evolved over millennia, although we have a tendency to consider them to be recent. Man, considered a 'super predator' has eliminated many mammal species. Using gun and axe he combines direct destruction with the degradation of habitats. The action of carnivores, which capture their prey in nature is very different. Even so in zones not marked by the presence of man the quantity of prey varies from year to year. Climate, for example, can modify plant productivity which in turn influences the numbers of herbivores, and finally affect the numbers of carnivores. So relatively large changes in the density of animals, with time lags for different species, can be seen in the different levels of the food chain. It is even possible that some species can become locally extinct, but if there are relatives of these species living in the neighbourhood they may recolonise the area almost immediately. Such fluctuations have been studied in detail in many parts of Europe, especially the cyclical fluctuations of voles and their predators (birds and mammals) which follow them.

The regular analysis of rejection pellets of nocturnal raptors at a given site also demonstrates changes in the density of prey species.

Territory and movements

Each individual in a population of a species requires a certain space to fulfil its biological functions. The surface area of an animal's range can vary from a few square metres for a field vole to several square kilometres for the brown bear. There the animal finds food and shelter, meets other members of the species for reproduction and raises its young. It is usual to distinguish between the vital range (the space necessary for the individual to live) and the territory (the part of the living space actively defended by the individual against other members of the same species). Territories can be permanent or seasonal, defined geographically or they can be mobile (the space around an individual). The stag in rut roars to defend a small space where it assembles a herd of females and his territory can be both seasonal and mobile. Regularly inhabited and stable ranges are of interest to the observer because they normally require their inhabitants to leave marks. Some carnivores and rodents leave visible marks or scent traces, sometimes both, in strategic places and finding them is enough to indicate the presence of the species in an area. The faeces of carnivores are a characteristic marker.

A double dam built by beavers. An impressive structure.

A muskrat 'toilet' on the bank of a pond.   *The straight path of a fox in the snow.*

Social organisation

All species have some social life, though some are more inclined to be gregarious than others. In relatively solitary species contact may be maintained by indirect means, that is by odour or calls, but this does not mean that no social organisation exists.

The social base in mammals is usually a group comprising the female and young. In certain carnivores these are the only groupings found, with male and females meeting only briefly in the mating season. In mustelids, the male inhabits a territory which includes, in whole or in part, the territories of several females and the male may mate with any of the females. Rodents like the beaver or the marmot form social units depending on a reproductive pair (sometimes with two or three adult females) accompanied by the young of the year or the two preceding years. Ungulates live usually in single sex herds, and pairs or harems only form in the mating season.

The young can become independent at various ages depending on the species (three weeks, on average, in small rodents, two or three years in bears). In general the young males move further from the family group than the females which may stay longer with their mother, as in foxes and ungulates. But these behaviour patterns are rarely fixed. The fox, for example, depending on the available food resources, can live alone in many hectares of open country or in family groups at the edges of large towns.

Reproduction and population dynamics

Each species faces conditions, often unfavourable, that can lead to the disappearance of some individuals (absence of food, predation, movement to seek new territory). The production of new generations replaces their losses.

For small rodents the cycle of the replacement of generations, when circumstances are favourable, is fast and there may be a rapid increase in the population. When the field vole, the bank vole and the water vole live close together they may demonstrate totally independent cycles of abundance, usually every three or four years. On the other hand female bats seldom give birth to more than one young each year so bat populations do not show the same violent fluctuations. The voles have a life expectancy of only months, the bats of several years. The longevity of some species compensates for their low reproductive rate, but they may be vulnerable to changes in the environment.

As for other species their population dynamics may be of the rodent type or of the bat type. For the weasels and stoats the size of the population depends on the quantity of prey available – their numbers are therefore linked to the number of rodents available.

LOOKING FOR MAMMALS

Finding mammals is not simply a matter of chance. Most of them live in particular habitats and are active at relatively regular times of day, year, life etc. Armed with this information we will have more chance of observing one or more species in the field.

WHERE: THE DIFFERENT TYPES OF HABITAT AND THE SPECIES FOUND

Although some species do not seem to show a particular preference for a specific habitat this is not so for the majority. Knowledge of the association between species and habitat makes the job of the observer simpler and often allows confirmation of the identity of an animal or of the source of the signs found in the field.

Grasslands and farmlands

In many European countries the natural habitats have almost disappeared; they have long since been replaced by cultivation, modified and remodified by generations of farmers. The vast grassland plains of today harbour some of the species linked to the original grasslands and some are secondarily adapted to these open habitats. Farmland is a highly modified habitat. Its slow development has allowed the installation of a rich fauna and flora, like wooded hedges, surrounding the grasslands and fields, which provide an environment similar to the woodland edges that separate the forest from the plains, a frontier zone (ecotone) where the species of the two habitats, open and closed, meet each other. The progressive expansion of farmland has considerable biological and economic effects.

Grasslands are the natural habitats of the field and common voles. Both live in comparable biotopes but where they live together the former is found in more humid areas, sometimes near hedges, while the latter is rarely found close to a wooded zone; the common vole is also the only species to colonise very open habitats such as the grasslands of polders.

The small rodents attract predators such as weasels and stoats. These animals use the grasslands as hunting grounds and the hedges for refuge. The shrews of the genus *Sorex* (e.g. the common shrew and Millets shrew) are also found in this type of habitat along with moles and water voles. In the vineyards of the south east of France, with a

Large deer thrive in lowland forests.

Mediterranean style of cultivation, enclosed by small walls, the lesser and pygmy white–toothed shrews are present.

The wide open spaces of cultivated plains, similar to the more easterly steppes, are the domain of the brown hare. Its running abilities are well adapted to the open habitat.

Forests and woodlands

The woodland zones are of several types depending on the species present, the altitude, the nature of the forest population (mature timber, plantation, etc.), the age of the formation and the density of the trees. All these aspects make the forest a complex environment and not as homogeneous as it at first appears. The monospecific cultures of a single age attract fewer species than more varied woodlands.

The forest may be a regular habitat or simply a refuge. The large ungulates need forests to provide calm protected shelters. This does not prevent them from emerging into the plains to seek food. The roe deer is clearly more emergent than the red deer and can be found in relatively small woods.

The small woodland rodents are typically represented by the wood mouse, the bank vole, the dormouse and the red and grey squirrels all

Mountains and cold regions have a specific fauna, including the ibex.

of which are capable of climbing. The limits marking the border between one habitat and the next are often difficult to discern. The wood mouse can be found on open ground while the bank vole makes use of the hedges to enter farmland. However, many species are particularly adapted to covered habitats. Small animals like the vole need less extensive cover than for example the deer.

The marten, much at ease in the forest, can capture squirrels and some birds (the woodpecker in particular) nesting in the cavities of trees. It also hunts on the ground. The lynx hunts on the ground capturing prey from rodents to small cervids. The wild cat evolved in the great forests where it is commonly found but curiously it is often seen hunting in open habitats.

Wetlands and rivers

Marshes, peat bogs, ponds and wide shallow estuaries are also frontier areas where land and water meet. Here too the biotopes are particularly rich but also fragile and much coveted by farmers. The extent of these habitats is diminishing and the species inhabiting them are in a vulnerable situation.

The rivers, from streams to the great rivers, form a network corresponding to ancient natural routes for the penetration of regions and habitats through connecting valleys. The mammals found in these habitats belong to all the groups. The modification of structure and behaviour linked to living in these habitats vary from one species to another but each type of adaptation is effective.

Of the insectivores, the water shrew lives close to open or running water whilst Miller's shrew prefers wet grasslands and meadows. The Pyrenees is the home of the desman, a type of water mole. Many rodents live near to water, for example the beaver and the water vole. Amongst the carnivores there are otters, mink and polecat. The last is less dependent on water than the other two species but is often found in wet habitats.

Several introduced species are also linked to water such as the muskrat, the coypu, the racoon, the American mink and the racoon dog. This may signify that the wet biotopes of Europe may have been under–exploited until recently or that such species adapt themselves particularly well to new habitats.

Mountains and cold regions

Since the glaciations of the Quaternary some particularly well adapted species have been able to survive on the edge of the ice sheet that once covered most of Europe. When the ice retreated these species moved north or were left behind on the tops of the great mountain ranges. The cold northern European zones of Iceland, Scandinavia and Scotland harbour a fauna quite different from that of the more southern areas. Reindeer, elk and musk ox disappeared long ago from the more southerly areas. As for the rodents the lemmings are characteristic of the tundra and taiga regions.

Some of the mountain chains such as the Alps and the Pyrenees provide, at their higher levels, living conditions similar to those of the tundra. Some species seem particularly faithful to these difficult conditions. They include the alpine shrew, the snow vole and the marmot as well as the variable hare. Each has a particular preference for a part of the habitat linked to rocks, alpine meadows or high forests.

Some species of ungulates live exclusively on mountains. The chamois, well adapted to snow is the most typical. The ibex, linked to rocky places, lives especially on rocks which are rapidly cleared of snow by the wind in winter and then on the high peaks in summer. The mouflon, which probably arrived in western Europe with man seems to prefer the mountain meadows. Its original biotope was probably much dryer than that currently found in western Europe.

Many carnivores are found on mountains although not exclusively linked to this habitat. For example the bear will also live on the plains and its Pyrenean refuge is simply an area of least disturbance. This is also the case for the lynx which is found in the Vosges, Jura and Pyrenean mountains where there are areas large enough, and with few people, to ensure its survival. This also explains why these species are vulnerable. They colonise the same sectors of mountains as man and their interests are divergent.

Towns and villages

Although some species disappear for ever on the arrival of man, others profit in various ways from the development of towns and villages. They are often species which live amongst rocks. Stone houses correspond, for these anthropophile species (those living near man), to an extension of their original natural biotope. This is the case with a number of bats (rhinolophs in particular). In other situations these bats would seek woodland nesting in the cavities of trees. Of the rodents, the dormouse is often found near houses, as are the house mouse and rats, which are ubiquitous but relatively dependent on towns at the northern limits of their range.

Towns also offer parks and gardens which attract many species normally living in farmland, grassland and forests. Squirrels quickly become tame if fed and not alarmed. Amongst the other groups of mammals the hedgehog, the mole (unhappily not much appreciated when discovered in our lawns) and even the roe deer will visit gardens at the edges of towns.

Some carnivores also invade the towns. The fox and the stone marten are two species that can adapt readily to urban conditions. The stone marten nests in the roofs of houses, sometimes quietly, sometimes more noisily especially while rearing a brood. The fox finds shelter below buildings or in abandoned or seldom used buildings.

Ubiquitous species

Mammals as a group are very adaptable animals. It is often difficult to establish clearly the type of habitat to which a particular species belongs and some species have very wide distributions. The larger carnivores and ungulates may pass through several habitats in the course of a single day.

It is impossible, therefore, to define the habitat of many species such as the house mouse, black rat, brown rat or fox. Such species are found almost everywhere and do not show clear preferences for particular habits. They demonstrate the great adaptability of mammals – they are opportunistic species.

WHEN: TIMES FOR OBSERVING AND FINDING SIGNS

Although the natural world is not precisely programmed, the lives of animals follow seasonal and diurnal rhythms, and physiological cycles. They are also sometimes affected by disturbance from exceptional circumstances. To be fruitful observations must take account of these events which determine to a large extent the lives of the animals.

The seasons

Seasonal rhythms provide the best background for watching the development of biological phenomena. Observations and the search for traces made through several seasons and over several years give a lot of interesting information.

Winter is perhaps the ideal season for the novice student to study mammals. Some species (e.g. hedgehog) will have hibernated, others have reduced activity (e.g. squirrels). Encounters are thus limited to a reduced number of species. The presence of snow is a helpful medium for learning to recognise species and their signs and to follow their movements, pursuits, hunts and meetings. The burrows of rodents and carnivores are also easier to find in winter as frost accumulates at the mouths of the burrows. The absence of vegetation allows a wider field of view plus there are fewer places for animals to hide.

The muskrat, a North American species, is well adapted to the rigours of winter.

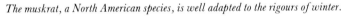

Nocturnal and very shy the badger is difficult to watch.

The spring is usually the period for births and for some species is also the mating season. The activities of March hares are well known and they can be seen cavorting in the green fields where cereals are growing. The animals are often so distracted by these activities that they are easy to observe. When the young are born new signs appear sometimes side by side with those of the adults. The young are often playful and inexperienced and are vulnerable to many dangers. They can also be found more easily than the adults.

In summer the nights are shorter and all species, even the most nocturnal, have a period of activity in daylight. It is therefore easier to see them at this time. It is also the period of reproduction for the roe deer and for the stone and beech martens. The baying of deer is often heard during this season.

In autumn in the great forests the noise of the red deer is a remarkable phenomenon. On mountains the jousts of the ibex and the chamois may be seen shortly after watching the marmots feverishly preparing their burrows for the winter. On the lowlands the squirrel buries nuts at the base of a tree and the bats gather insects to complete their reserves of fat for hibernation.

Day and night

Some species are almost completely nocturnal (bats) but most are active at dusk. Small mammals like shrews have periods of activity of only a few hours at a time, alternating with periods of rest throughout the 24 hours of the day. Many species are active at dawn and dusk (they are crepuscular), resting through the middle of both night and day. In areas where animals are often disturbed, more activity takes place at night. Traces and signs left by the animals are easily found by day but a mammalogist wishing to see the animals must go to bed late and rise early. At night many species are seen in the light of car headlamps.

The breeding season

Depending on the species, the gestation period, or whether there is direct or delayed implantation the breeding season can take place at any time of year. Often animals are more active during the breeding season, making significant movements or displays.

The roar of the red deer can be heard at the end of September and the beginning of October, the howling of foxes at the start of the year or the mating of the roe deer in summer. Hedgehogs, squirrels and marmots breed in spring with pursuits and remarkable display behaviours.

The mating of rodents and small insectivores, capable of reproducing several times a year, are much shorter and more difficult to see. Mating in carnivores is often accompanied by noise, as with foxes or martens, but is still difficult to observe. Often marking territories is more intense at this time and the traces are found more frequently.

Movements

Some territorial animals have little need to move. This is particularly the case for the females of some carnivores, ungulates and rodents. In contrast males are more often on the move. In the ungulates (e.g. deer, chamois, ibex) adult males gather a group of females for mating. The carnivores do the same and some individuals are capable of dispersing over large distances to find a mate.

There are other circumstances in which an animal finds itself outside its vital range; this is the period when the young gain independence. Here too the young males are greater wanderers than the females, on average moving much further.

Other circumstances aiding observation

The keen observer must know how to profit from any unusual circumstances that modify the behaviour of animals which may make them easier to see. A flooding river, for example, drives out the fauna from its banks and the animals may be found on nearby high ground. The lives of the animals in such circumstances are usually additionally threatened because they are displaced into the territories of their neighbours who will defend their homes. Agricultural activities, building works and fire may also expose individual animals or their traces which would otherwise remain hidden. In periods of drought bats may fly during the day to find water and many other species may concentrate their activities near drinking places.

DIRECT OBSERVATION

HIDES AND CAMOUFLAGE

Mammals are shy and therefore difficult to observe. Many only emerge at night or dusk. Some may occasionally be seen by chance but, to watch them regularly, it is important to construct a hide or at least some sort of good camouflage. Compared to birds, sight is not the best developed sense in mammals, even so the hide should be positioned so that it avoids detection through hearing or odour.

When there is no wind or it is in a favourable direction, perfect immobility is sufficient camouflage as long as the silhouette of the observer or the colour of his clothing does not contrast with the environment.

In the forest the observer may stand behind or beside a tree but if the background is open it is preferable to lie on the ground or even better to be covered by a dull coloured net. This type of camouflage is usually enough if one is observing rodents (e.g. voles, rats, squirrels, marmots, coypu, muskrat, beaver etc.). Successful observation depends largely on having the patience to stay in hiding for a long time. It is preferable in most cases to remain at a distance from the subject and to scrutinise the area using binoculars.

To see more secretive animals it is necessary to construct a simple portable hide. Four stakes in metal or wood linked by cross pieces to make the structure rigid and a net covering is sufficient. The hide should merge into the environment wherever possible and should be set up several days prior to the observation period so that the animals can become accustomed to its presence. Observation may be assisted by placing bait at a distance from the hide. It is important to remember that a hide must *not* cause any serious disturbance to the animal.

The track of a hare in snow.

PHOTOGRAPHY AND FILM

The success of still and cine–photography of animal life depends on ensuring that the animals are not disturbed, particularly when operating close to their shelters or nests. A sudden movement risks disturbing the parents which may lead them to abandon the young. Too many bird nests are lost in this way and the same problem applies to mammals.

Two pieces of equipment are particularly useful for photographing mammals and their traces: a powerful telephoto lens to take photographs of individual animals, and a close-up lens to photograph traces and tracks.

If photographing faeces or footprints it is usual to double the field of view and to include a scale. Traces often lack colour or relief and are frequently found in dark places so the use of flash is important.

The noise from the exposure often causes the animals to flee so wrapping the camera in a sound–muffling material is recommended.

To obtain good results with cine–photography it is necessary to work in 16 mm minimum but the equipment and cost is beyond most amateurs. However the development of video cameras can give good pictures although the range of optics in this medium is still limited.

One of the authors, Christian Bouchardy, searching for indications of the presence of otters along a deep running stream.

A Brown or European hare at its nest. Hidden in the grass it can be difficult to see.

CAPTURING MAMMALS

Small mammals are difficult to follow in their natural habitat. In some cases keeping them in captivity is essential in order to study their behaviour and physiology. However, first one must learn to catch them . . .

Methods

There are many different types of small mammal traps – a buried jam pot alongside a wall, metal corridor traps, and a variety of commercially available rat traps, all with their advantages and disadvantages. Their size and the placement in different habitats determines the species caught. Traps are needed to complete an inventory of a particular region or to search specifically for a particular species. Not all small mammals show the same behaviour towards traps, some being more difficult to trap than others. Subterranean species are more difficult to catch.

Precautions

The objective is to catch live individuals and some rules need to be observed. Animals are found dead in traps, particularly metal traps, due to poor thermal insulation. Most traps can be adapted by adding a wooden container which gives shelter and by providing nourishment in case of cold or intense heat.

It is also necessary to visit traps frequently and not to leave them set if they cannot be visited within half a day if trapping rodents or within an hour or two for shrews. Pitfall traps should be covered if rain is expected.

Protected species

Whether the study is motivated by scientific research or simply an interest in mammals, it must be remembered that certain species are protected by law. Most European countries now have laws protecting certain species and the student must obtain permission from the scientific and management authorities which exist in each country. It is important to notice that even small species may be protected including shrews, hedgehogs, bats and some rodents.

Traps are rarely specific to a species, a weasel or a shrew can both be caught in rodent traps.

Rearing in captivity

Before attempting to keep animals in captivity it is essential to study their biology and needs. A lot of information on, for example, shrews has been gleaned from studying the living animals in captivity. It seemed impossible to keep these animals in captivity until the work of an English zoologist, Dr Peter Crowcroft in the fifties. His skill and talent led to the discovery of the keys to raising them. He also estab- lished that common and pygmy shrews could live together.

In general the herbivorous and granivorous species (rodents) are easier to feed and keep in captivity than the insectivores because the latter require a supply of live prey (grasshoppers, flour beetles). Some insectivores will eat commercial preparations such as pet foods. It is good to vary the diet. A single regime may not include all the nutrients required by the animal and may lead to vitamin or mineral deficien- cies or excesses.

Some species will reproduce in captivity. For the raising of the young to be achieved satisfactorily, the environmental conditions must be right (isolation of females, good food for adults to give satis- factory lactation, etc.).

It must also be borne in mind that the confinement of many animals in a small space may lead to illness through parasitic and infectious diseases.

The reconstruction of biotopes

To study small mammals one can either capture individuals and raise them in captivity or else try to arrange the habitat and surroundings, in a garden, to attract them to areas where they can be seen say from the window of a study. These arrangements are not always simple but they can lead to satisfying results.

If one is interested in bats one might be able to install well pro- tected nestboxes or allow them entry to aerated lofts or small spaces between stones or tiles (in places where the colonies will not be dis- turbed at the breeding season).

In the garden it is preferable to leave for as long as possible old hollow trees. Instead of planting many exotic species plant European species of trees and shrubs (hazelnut, fruit trees – one may even eat some of the fruit) or indigenous conifers for squirrels in accordance with the regional climate and the type of soil. Birds will also app- reciate such gardens.

Watering places play an important role as long as they do not become traps. Artificial basins with smooth sides if not totally full may lead to drowning. Stones, grilles or rafts will allow safe access to the water.

Heaps of wood, stones or leaves left for the winter and spring will also attract small mammals.

Radio–tracking

To close this chapter on direct observation, we should note that scientists have for some years been using a very precise method – radio–tracking – for following mammals in their natural habitat. The principle is simple: an animal is captured and fitted with a very small transmitter and battery. With the aid of a listening system the signal is detected, localised and the movements and daily rhythms of the animal are recorded. For a long time this technique was restricted to animals of large or medium size but now thanks to miniaturisation the movements of small mammals can also be studied with radios weighing only a few grams.

Indications of Presence in the Field

Droppings

The word droppings includes all types of excrement left by mammals but other words are commonly used for certain species e.g. otter 'spraints'.

When droppings are found it is neccessary to examine the form and dimensions, the colour and brightness, the consistency, the smell and the composition. Details can be found in the species accounts and the summary table is designed to help preliminary identification. It is important not to handle faeces left by mammals. The usual method is to lift them with the aid of a plastic bag used as a glove. Very serious illness may be contracted from direct handling as droppings may harbour parasites, most of which are not visible to the naked eye.

The smell of droppings is an important element in their identification (see the section on odours) but again caution is neccessary during examination. The colour and consistency of droppings vary considerably for the same animal depending on the food eaten.

The most important characteristics for identifying droppings are the size and general appearance. Using these two characters it is possible to identify the family of the species and often the species to which the animal belongs. There is little in common between the small round droppings of the hare or rabbit and the small cylindrical ones of the vole, muskrat or coypu and the twisted, long thin droppings of small carnivores.

When the samples appear similar in shape and composition, the dimensions are useful for identification. It is relatively simple, for example, to identify, from size, the droppings of the rabbit and hare, or the vole and muskrat. Some difficulties arise when the size and diet of species are similar. It is difficult to distinguish the droppings of a large stoat from those of a small polecat. There is no scientific means to identify droppings at the species level but it is possible to be nearly certain in many cases. Above all a good knowledge of the terrain is helpful. The animals do not leave their droppings at random. Amongst the carnivores for instance droppings serve for marking territory. They are therefore deposited at strategic places and regularly used points. The place of deposition, a stone, a tuft of grass, a run and the immediate environment may give useful information about the identity of the animal which lives there.

FOOTPRINTS

The footprints of mammals fall into two separate groups – those which show hoofs and those showing feet and claws. When footprints of non–hoofed mammals are examined the principal characters are claw marks, digital pads, the plantar pad and carpal pads. Digital pads number four or five and the plantar pad can be a single block or multilobed. The carpal pads seen in a few species are behind the anterior pads and seldom appear in prints. The plantar pad is usually broader than long but in certain species it can be longer in the hind footprint when the animal supports itself on its heels and the plantar pad imprints fully, as in the otter or the bear. The claw mark is more or less visible depending on the nature of the terrain; in some animals the claws are retractile, as in the cat or the lynx and are never seen in footprints. The feet of mammals adapted to water, like the coypu, the otter and the beaver have webs which can be seen on the most complete prints.

The measurements given in this book are taken from the border of the most anterior digital pad to the base of the plantar pad without taking claws into account.

The imprints of hooved species consist of two parallel 'slots', although in truth the animals have four digits, the 'slots' belong to the two central digits. The lateral digits situated higher up the leg seldom appear in the prints except when the mud is very deep or the animal has jumped. The lateral digits of the roe deer (dew claws) are often

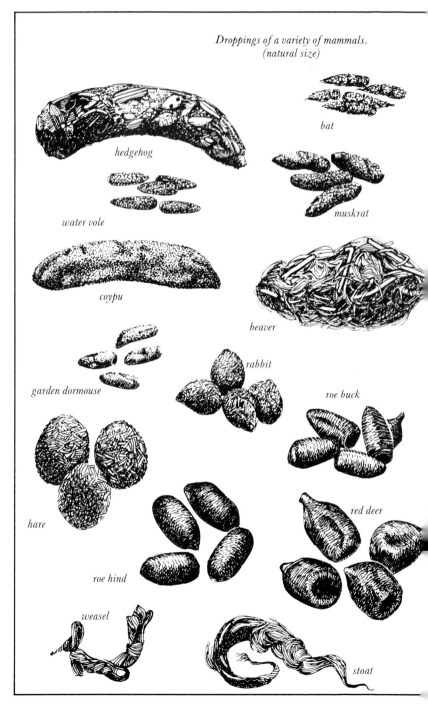

Droppings of a variety of mammals.
(natural size)

bat

hedgehog

water vole

muskrat

coypu

beaver

garden dormouse

rabbit

roe buck

hare

red deer

roe hind

weasel

stoat

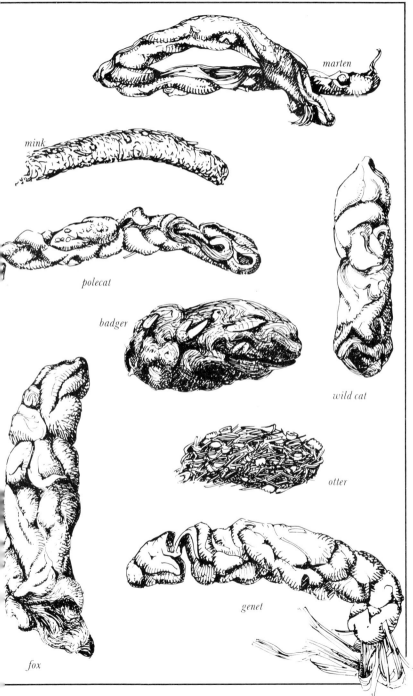

marten

mink

polecat

badger

wild cat

otter

genet

fox

visible and allow the identification of the species because they make the print wider. The measurements given in this book do not include the exterior digits.

In specialised works data are given for the position of the pads in different gaits (walk, trot, gallop, bound). But experience in the field shows that the track of an animal is very variable and changeable and it is rare to be able to read the traces for a sufficient distance. If this type of observation is characteristic of a species the information is included in the species accounts under 'indications of presence'. Description and measurements of footprints are also given for each species described.

The search for prints

Trackers who live in regions regularly covered with snow will quickly get excellent results. Nothing is easier than to follow the tracks of an animal in the snow. This may give rise to the saying 'the snow is the book of the soul'. Correct reading of tracks is usually only possible in good conditions. It is important to inspect the prints quickly before fresh snowfalls and it must be remembered that in snow the tracks are usually larger than the prints left by an animal in mud. If the snowfall has stopped and no more is reported you must hurry out to prospect for tracks early the next morning. This gives the best chance of discovering any traces of animal activity during the night – emergence from the nest, hunting, resting places, dropping sites, return to burrows, etc.

When there is no snow it is best to search places where the earth, the sand and the mud are bare of vegetation: under bridges, on river banks and pondsides, at the edge of these and in estuaries at low tide,

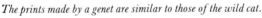
The prints made by a genet are similar to those of the wild cat.

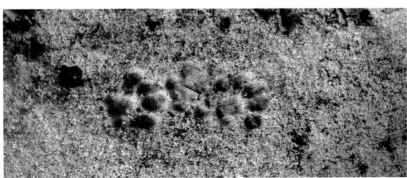

near streams and on muddy roads. If the route an animal usually takes is well known it is possible to make an artificial mud patch using fine sand or wet soil. To encourage the animal to show, some bait – vegetable or meat – can be placed near the area. As soon as a track is found the maximum information should be noted and if possible a drawing or a photograph should be made. To avoid errors it is necessary to become familiar with the tracks made by domestic animals and pets which surround us (cats, dogs, pigs, sheep, etc.). As soon as the shape of some prints are known one can easily identify new ones by a process of elimination.

The drawings given in this book are of the best, most complete prints which are unfortunately only rarely found in the field. That is

The print of the forefoot of a badger; the claws make clear marks.

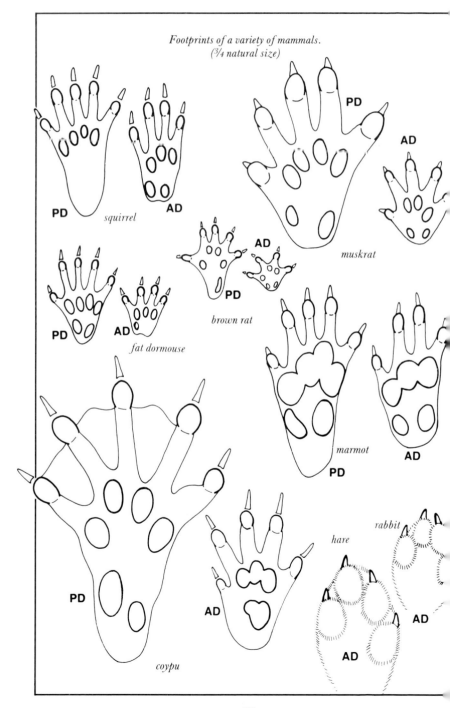

Footprints of a variety of mammals.
(¾ natural size)

squirrel

muskrat

fat dormouse

brown rat

marmot

coypu

hare

rabbit

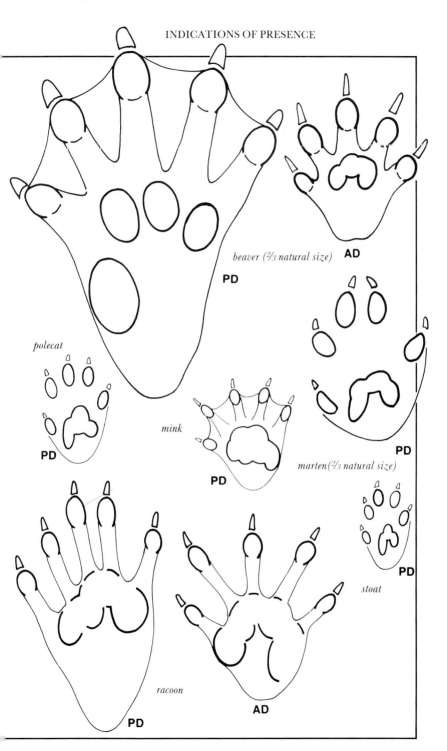

beaver (⅔ natural size) **AD**

PD

polecat

PD

mink

PD

marten (⅔ natural size)

PD

stoat

PD

racoon

PD

AD

why the reader, having discovered a print must be careful not to jump to conclusions but must try to obtain supplementary information to confirm the identification.

THE TRAILS

Trails, or runs, are the paths made by the habitual comings and goings of the animals. They only appear where regularly used, which suggests that they have some strategic importance for the animal that makes them. The most characteristic trails begin at a nest or burrow and lead to areas of feeding or hunting or mark the edge of a territory. Their appearance varies considerably depending on the season and the nature of the ground. They can also be used by several species, which does not make identification easy. In this case it is better to search for other indications, which may be near the path – prints, droppings, hairs, nests, or burrows.

Take for example a run found along the edge of a river in the reeds. It may be used by the coypu, muskrat, otter or mink or by a variety of small mammals such as the water vole. But it is possible also that only one of the species actually made the track. The general shape, its position in the area and length do not give enough information. The run should be followed to find supplementary information. If the run is used by an otter, droppings will be left at each end where the track enters the water. A coypu and a muskrat will leave easily identifiable droppings, moreover they will both cut the reeds at their base which

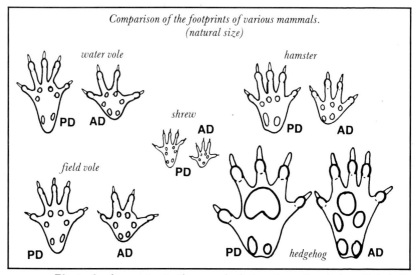

Comparison of the footprints of various mammals.
(natural size)

water vole

hamster

shrew

field vole

hedgehog

The track of a marten in the snow leads to a tree where it has climbed. ▶

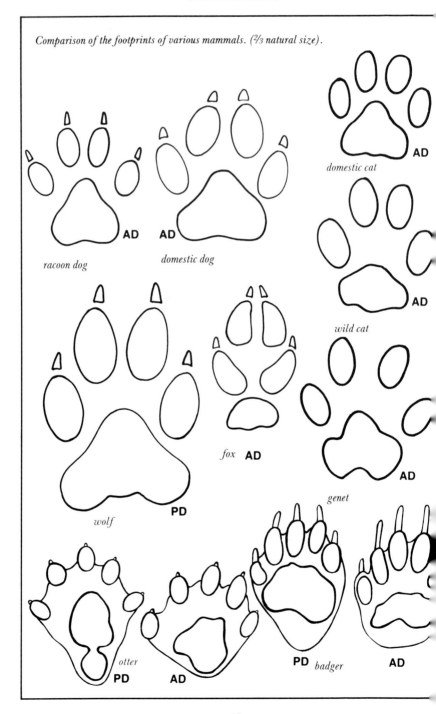

Comparison of the footprints of various mammals. (⅔ natural size).

racoon dog

domestic dog

domestic cat **AD**

wild cat **AD**

wolf **PD**

fox **AD**

genet **AD**

otter **PD** **AD**

PD badger **AD**

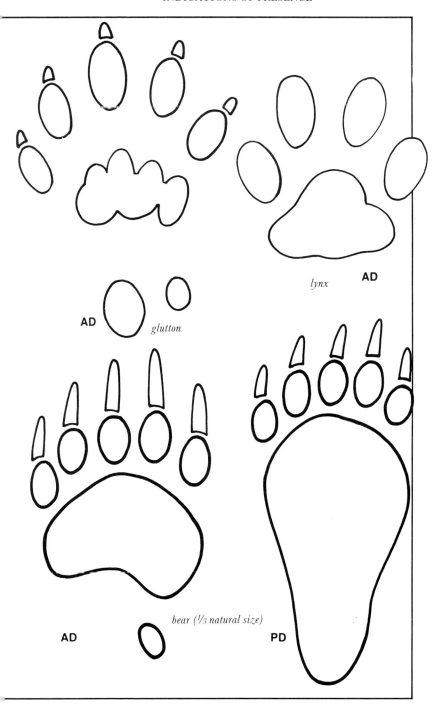

lynx **AD**

AD *glutton*

bear (¹/₃ natural size)

AD

PD

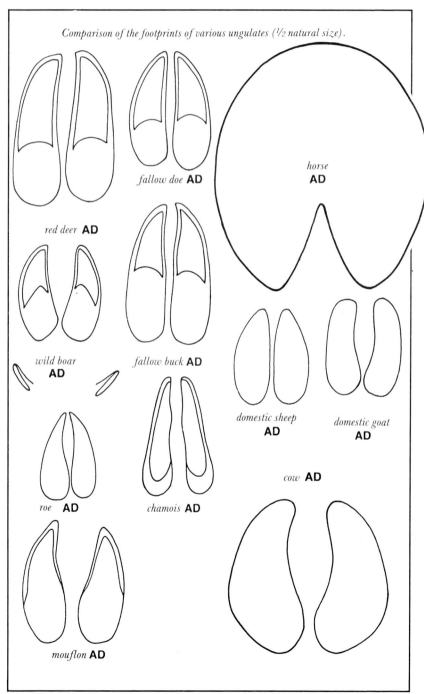

Comparison of the footprints of various ungulates (½ natural size).

horse
AD

fallow doe **AD**

red deer **AD**

fallow buck **AD**

wild boar
AD

domestic sheep
AD

domestic goat
AD

roe **AD**

chamois **AD**

cow **AD**

mouflon **AD**

The star shaped prints of a muskrat. ▶

the otter does not do. The track of a water vole is only a few centimetres wide while that of a muskrat is about 20 cm and that of a coypu up to 30 cm wide.

Tracks are particularly easy to find amongst dead leaves and low vegetation. On sloping terrain they make a road that follows the contours of the land. On the dew covered grass, an animal leaves in its wake a deep, easily seen furrow. Some aquatic mammals, notably the beaver, the muskrat and the coypu make tracks in vegetation that fill with water to make small canals. The tracks of red deer and roe deer which lead to wallows are so big and so well defined that they may appear man–made. The fox and the badger are so faithful to their tracks that it is relatively simple to follow them to the den.

In grassland, one can often see a multitude of small tracks measuring 3–5 cm wide, which lead to burrow entrances. This is generally the work of voles which stay in the shelter of the tunnels whilst on the move and can regain their nests in case of danger. When the tracks are made under snow they become full of earth and vegetation and after the snow melts they resemble long sinuous sausages. Tracks hidden in long grass become visible as paths of green when the grass withers in autumn.

These examples serve to demonstrate how much tracks vary between species and that there is no simple key to their identification. Trackers must construct their own scheme depending on the terrain and the animals known to live there.

FOOD REMAINS

When a carnivore catches its prey it usually devours it at once and entire. If it is too big it may not be completely eaten. The abandoned remains can give information about the prey and the predator. The best way, for example, to make a list of small mammals present in an area is not to catch them, a long and difficult task, but to analyse the rejection pellets of birds of prey (the raptors) as they are much better hunters than humans.

Feathers and partly eaten bodies of birds are often found in the field. To find out whether the predator is a mammal or a raptor it is necessary to look at the state of feathers. Those which have been killed by a sparrowhawk or a goshawk are intact whilst those killed by a fox or a marten, which grab their prey with their teeth, have torn and cut ends to the feathers. It is less easy to find the remains of meals of carnivores that take their prey to the den or a quiet place to eat.

Many mammals make stores of food – animal or vegetable. The water vole buries considerable quantities of bulbs and roots in a burrow near to its nest. Many voles do the same and other less provident animals profit from the stores. The bear appreciates, in spring, the bulbs hidden by voles. The voles may compensate for this by discovering the cache of nuts hidden by a squirrel.

The weasel, polecat and beech marten take advantage of plagues of rodents to gather reserves for bad times. If you discover a pile of dead rats in the straw of a barn it is possible that a beech marten lives in the vicinity. This species also likes eggs, abandoning the carefully cleaned shells at the entrance to its burrow. When a carnivore or a hedgehog finds an egg it partly breaks it by digging a hole in the side before swallowing the contents.

The remains of meals give clear, precise information about the prey but one must be more cautious about the identity of the predator. Workers who find a fish partly eaten on a river bank nearly always attribute the kill to an otter but experience shows that an identical kill can be found where there are no otters. The fish may have been the victim of an osprey or a heron. The body of a roe deer, mouflon or even a sheep is not necessarily the work of lynx, wolf of bear which are now rare. Feral dogs, which are in no danger of extinction, may be to blame.

TRACES ON VEGETATION

Cereal crops have always attracted both small and large mammals. The recent rapid expansion of maize growing in Europe has served to increase this phenomenon. In a single field of maize many traces can be found especially if the field is bordered by water.

Several species of mammal attack cereals by cutting the stems in order to reach the ears. Voles and hamsters cut the stems a few centimetres above ground. The muskrat and the coypu cut them at an angle whilst sitting on their haunches – the cuts are found at 20 cm from the ground for the former and about 40–50 cm for the latter. The badger and the roe deer crush the cereals down to the ground to reach the ears and can damage the crop over many square metres. Red deer crush cereals under foot and can also break them down when arranging a place to lie. Between the rows of crops, it is possible to see many footprints and droppings left by several other mammal species. The association of these and the preceding indications will often aid in the identification of the animals that have passed through a field.

At the edge of bodies of water, tufts of reeds are often found cut into pieces 2–10 cm long. The green outer part has been eaten and only the white medulla is found in the remains of the meal. This is the work of aquatic rodents, mainly the muskrat and amphibious vole.

TRACES ON FRUIT

The squirrel and the wood mouse are fond of conifer seeds but each uses a different technique to extract them from their scaly protection. The squirrel collects the cone from the tree and bites off the scales as it sits on a branch or at an eating place, on a tree stump for example, to extract the seeds. The cones eaten by a squirrel have a characteristic irregular frayed appearance, and often the scales are not completely severed from the central core. The wood mouse is only interested in fallen cones like those dropped by a squirrel and eats them tidily. They are cleaned smoothly to the base. In both cases the tips of the cones where there are no seeds are left intact.

The work of the squirrel and of other rodents when eating hazelnuts is equally characteristic. The squirrel opens the nuts in two equal parts. It holds the nut with its upper incisors whilst digging a small hole at the end with the lower incisors then it slides a tooth into the hole and cuts the nut in two by pressure of its jaws. Small rodents cut a circular hole in the shell, holding the nut in their forefeet. The same technique is used for fruit seeds which may be found heaped on stones or outside the opening to the burrow.

Orchards are particularly attractive to the dormouse and the garden dormouse which eat the fruit either while it is still on the tree or in the storehouse after the harvest.

TRACES ON TREES AND BRANCHES

Rodents, deer and lagomorphs leave numerous traces on trunks, branches and shoots of trees when they scratch, bark or gnaw. After a wallow red and roe deer scratch vigorously against nearby trees so that the sap mixes with the mud and hairs.

At the time of antler growth deer rub vigorously on trees to remove the velvet covering the new antlers. This is noticeable during March and April for the roe deer, in July for the red deer and in September for the fallow deer. Three months later the deer are again attacking the trees, this time at the rut. Red and roe deer bark young trees longitudinally leaving long scars of several dozen centimetres. In winter they feed on the bark as a supplement when food is scarce.

Many rodents also attack the bark of trees and their roots. The water vole can cause the death of large trees by gnawing the roots. Hares, rabbits, muskrats, coypu and small voles bark trees at the base especially in winter and spring. The squirrel and bank vole, which climbs well can attack the bark of branches.

The young shoots of conifers are much appreciated by the mouflon

Wild pigs and deer often scratch on the same tree after a mud bath. Their black and brown hairs are found at different heights on the trunk.

and the roe deer, damaging the growing tips and so causing great damage to forests. The trees pruned in this way grow in width and take on a characteristic bushy shape.

SCRAPES, SCRATCHES AND STORES

Almost all the scrapes seen on the ground are the result of animals searching for food. Many mammals scrape in snow, in grass, in piles of leaves and in soil to find the larvae of insects, roots, bulbs or fruit. The wood mice, voles, squirrels and dormice make many scrapes when they are searching for hazelnuts, beech nuts, acorns, chestnuts and other dry fruits that have fallen to the ground. The badger, the fox, the genet, the polecat, the bear and the dog, dig deep holes in their attempts to unearth voles or wood mice.

In winter when the ground is covered with snow or is frozen, the deer scrape with their hooves to find grass. Hares and rabbits also make scrapes, beside which they often leave droppings. The badger is especially good at making scrapes, leaving them along its trails and through its territory. It digs up the nests of wasps and ants, and opens old nests where many succulent larvae are found. It works in the same

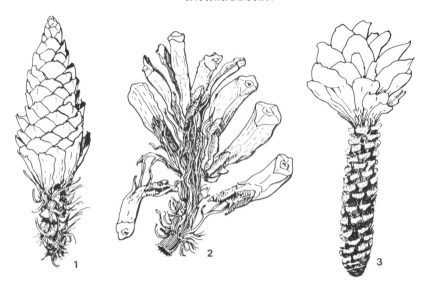

Remains of meals: 1 Green pine cone eaten by a squirrel; 2 Pine cone decorticated by a squirrel; 3 A ripe cone gnawed by a wood mouse.

way as the wild boar although digging less deeply than the latter which opens short furrows, using its snout to search for roots, acorns or small animals. These furrows may be up to 25 cm deep and may contain in places a sort of roll of grass or soil. The badger makes some scrapes for the disposal of droppings, these are the 'pots' which in a group form the toilet.

Scratches are found more rarely and are mostly visible on trunks and branches of trees. These are made by wild cats, sharpening their claws and by martens and squirrels. The broad traces of parallel scratches left by the bear do not have a known function, but some scientists think that they play a role in territorial marking.

WALLOWS AND NESTS

The roe and red deer habitually roll in mud or dust in particular places that may be frequented for several years. These big depressions at the edge of marshes, ponds and wet ditches are called wallows. When the ground water is not deep the wallows can be found anywhere in the forest – they grow deeper bath by bath. The foot-prints and body impressions can be clearly seen in the mud. Nearby trees show marks where the animals have rubbed after a bath. It is probable that the deer and the wild boar roll in the mud either to get rid of parasites or to protect against them. The sites of wallows should not be confused with resting places, which are dry and less deep although the ground in them may be bare.

Hares do not dig holes like rabbits. They rest in a nest, a slight depression about 30 cm wide hidden by a tuft of grass or a bush. In general these nests are not deep and are found in the shelter of a bush, an overhang of earth, or under the low branches of a tree. The roe deer likes to bed down under young spruce trees or under holly bushes. It scrapes the soil easily and the nest can be clearly seen amongst the grass or dead leaves which surround it. The bed of a wild boar is less well arranged than the one made by the sow in which she gives birth to her young.

Many mammals that live in holes in the ground or in hollow trees also use nests in the open particularly in summer, notably the genet, the marten, the fox, the otter and the weasel. The genet and the wild cat make their nests several metres above the ground, in the heart of an ivy plant or in the fork of a branch. Aquatic rodents make beds in the open on heaps of reeds or rushes. The size of the bed and the droppings nearby usually aid in identifying the species.

HOLES AND TUNNELS

With the exception of species that construct aerial nests, such as the squirrel, various dormice, the harvest mouse and the black rat, rodents are all excellent diggers. They find underground a shelter offering great security and, for some, important food resources. A large number of insectivores and carnivores also live in tunnels, which are used by less able but opportunistic diggers such as the polecat, the wild cat, the otter, the genet, the European and American minks and the marten.

The inside of the burrow remains hidden. It is principally the entrances, the start of the tunnels and the heaps of debris which give useful indications as to the identity of the occupant. There are three main types of burrow: those dug by animals of small size, those found near water or on river banks and those found in grassland or in forest. It is difficult to differentiate between the burrows of the various small mammals. Moreover, other indications such as droppings and tracks are also very similar and a simple method of identification is not available. In truth the best way of determining the occupant of a hole is to place a trap in front of the entrance. The work of the mole and that of the water vole are very similar as both dig tunnels (see species descriptions).

As for the tunnels found in grasslands or forests the indications are given in the species descriptions – mainly in the text devoted to the fox, the badger and the racoon dog. The diameter of the opening and the form of the discarded soil can provide clues to the identification of the inhabitant as long as one bears in mind the possibility of cohabitation and appropriation. The hole of a badger or a fox is usually easy to identify but a polecat can be found in a rabbit hole, a weasel or a stoat in that of a vole, an otter, a wild cat, a marten or a genet in a badger or fox hole. The best example of cohabitation comes from Scotland where it is recorded that in the same system of tunnels there lived a fox, a badger, an otter and a rabbit – a fact authenticated by radio–tracking. To measure correctly the diameter of the entrance of a burrow it is neccessary to push the measure a little way into the burrow because most entrances form a funnel, being wider near the outside. The tunnel of a badger measures 30 cm in diameter, that of the fox 20–25 cm and that of a rabbit 10–15 cm.

The banks of rivers offer a great variety of holes and tunnels dug by mammals from the Pyrenean desman to the beaver, including the water shrew, the water vole, the brown rat, the mink, the muskrat, the otter and the coypu. The tunnel of a shrew measures less than 5 cm in diameter, that of the water vole 5–8 cm and those of the polecat, the mink and the muskrat 10–15 cm. The larger holes, those of the coypu and the beaver can reach a diameter over 30 cm.

The hole of a coypu.

Hairs

The tufts of hair left here and there by small mammals are not the best indicators of presence as they are rarely found and difficult to identify but they are useful in confirming the presence, or to start the observer on the track of more evidence. The passageways under fences, places of rest, runs, bathing places and toilets are the principal places where animals lose hairs.

When following the path of an animal it helps to pay close attention to places where an obstacle bars the path, such as barbed wire, on which tufts of hair are often left, or some dense bushes consisting of brambles or thorns. If a nest or resting place is discovered, hairs may be found by careful examination of the bottom of the bed. The presence of hairs can confirm that it is really a place where a small mammal has rested. Runs are used by aquatic animals to leave the water to dry their fur. The hairs they lose by rolling on their backs and grooming are easily visible on packed snow especially those of the otter and the polecat.

Several species have the habit of rubbing against a tree to remove the mud after a wallow in the dirt or simply to scratch as do cows and horses. Many hairs are found stuck to the bark or caught in the resin of trees wounded by repeated rubbing by for example the bears and the red and roe deer. Near wallows used by the roe and the red deer

A rabbit warren in the open on sandy ground.

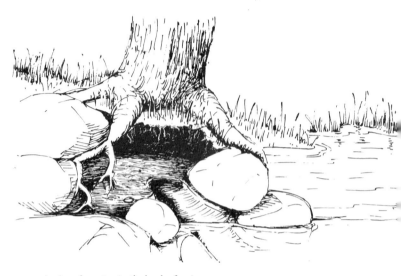

Entrance to the den of an otter in the bank of a river.

hairs can be found on the tree trunks – the hairs of the roe at about
1 m from the ground and those of the red a little higher. Long rough
black hairs of the roe deer also carpet the sides of the hollows where
they wallow.

The length and colour of the hairs allow a few species to be identified by the naked eye. When large black and white hairs are found on
a barbed wire fence it is almost certain that a badger has passed that
way. The hairs of a bear caught on a tree trunk are also characteristic.
But for most mammals identification to species by this means remains
difficult. Only a few specialists are able to do this by studying three
major characters of hair under the microscope – the structure of the
medulla, the form of the transverse section and the type of scales
covering the hair. A reference collection of hairs can be simply made
by removing a few hairs from known animals either captives or
specimens found dead.

Odour

Most amateur mammalogists are, like ornithologists, accustomed to
using eyes and ears to seek the animals. Compared to that of other
mammals the human sense of smell is poorly developed and relatively
little exploited. Experience shows that a good tracker must also make

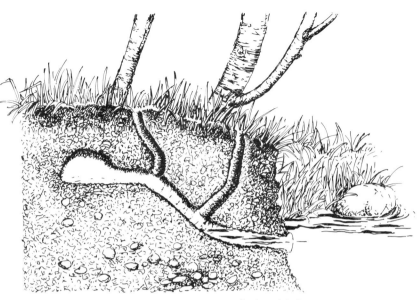

Section of the burrow of a water vole.

use of his sense of smell. Occasionally the smell of a mammal will be detected by chance during a walk. Most often it is the smell of a fox, sometimes a mustelid, but this type of information is too ephemeral to help seriously with the study of mammals. The smell emanating from a burrow or nest may be more significant. It helps to establish whether a hole is inhabited or not or to discover an entrance amongst rocks where debris and tracks are missing.

It is not possible here to give a list of odours emitted by mammals, their urine or their droppings. Our vocabulary is insufficient to describe the subtleties and nuances. Although the sense of smell in humans is less acute than that in a dog it is possible with a little experience to determine which species is using a hole (fox, rabbit, badger, genet, otter, etc.). The droppings of an animal will give out a scent that varies according to the diet, whether vegetable or carrion, and the droppings of many animals have similar scents. Some people profess to be able to distinguish the difference between the scents of the droppings of closely related species such as the beech marten and the stone marten. This type of ability is perhaps a little suspect. However if one has a good knowledge of the species present in an area it is possible to recognise, by elimination, the scent of the droppings of several species – the scent of otter droppings is sweet, whilst that of the polecat is sickening even if the two have eaten similar food.

Rodent droppings have little odour, which lasts for only a short time, the same applies to the droppings of deer and the guano of bats.

In addition to the smell from the remains of food many species also produce characteristic scents from various glands.

CRIES AND NOISES

Compared to other groups such as birds and frogs, mammals are relatively silent. They only disclose their presence at certain times of year or in circumstances linked to particular behavioural activities. Communication between individuals is more often through odour than through sound.

Some characteristic sounds can identify some unseen species especially in the breeding season, during combat or when an animal gives the alarm. The roar of a red deer and the howl of a wild cat are sounds produced in the breeding season. By howling the wolves gather together and form packs. The baying of a roe deer and the whistling of a marmot are usually signals of danger. The marmots are amongst the few animals more easily found by sound than sight.

During movement and hunting mammals emit sounds which help to detect them. The most favourable times to hear these noises are during the night. Seated in a quiet place all sorts of noises can be heard. This is the best technique for finding small mammals like hedgehogs, shrews or rodents which scratch amongst dead leaves.

REMAINS OF ANIMALS

As well as the remains of a meal – the result of predation – corpses, bones and other remains are often found in the field whether as a result of natural or accidental death. Deer lose their antlers each year, some time after the rut. The reindeer male loses his antlers in winter whilst the antlers of the female are lost later in the spring. In other species only the males carry antlers and these fall in February or March for the red deer, April or May for the fallow, and October or November for the elk. The discovery of a set of antlers is always an interesting moment for the naturalist especially if rodents seeking calcium have left their marks on the surface.

Complete bodies are frequently discovered along roadsides where thousands of animals are killed each year. Although this manner of collecting is tragic it gives much useful information about the fauna of the locality. The search for road casualties should be done on foot as many corpses are thrown into ditches.

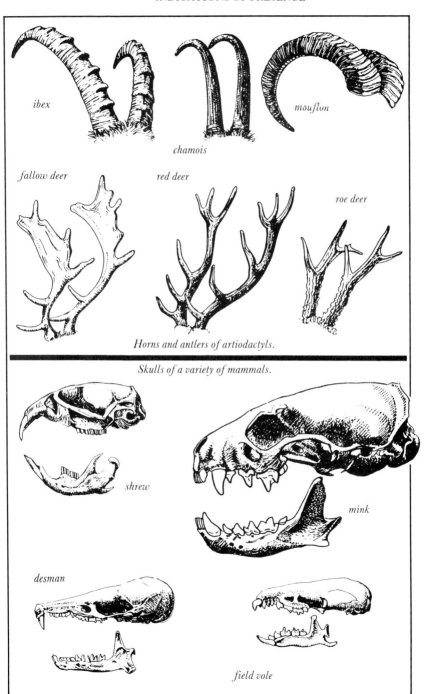

ibex

chamois

mouflon

fallow deer

red deer

roe deer

Horns and antlers of artiodactyls.

Skulls of a variety of mammals.

shrew

mink

desman

field vole

NESTS

Many mammals construct nests more or less underground and these can be in a chamber of their burrow, in a tuft of grass or a heap of stones or other shelter. These are principally carnivores, rodents and insectivores. Other species have aerial nests high in the branches of trees like birds. The squirrel, the harvest mouse and the dormouse are specialists in aerial nests. Nests which are good indicators of presence are described in the species accounts.

The largest nest, that built by the squirrel, has a diameter of about 20–50 cm; the next largest are those of the fat dormouse and the garden dormouse (10–20 cm in diameter). These nests are made of grass, twigs, leaves and moss.

The presence of fresh green vegetation in a nest is a good indication of the presence of the builder. The squirrel, fat dormouse and garden dormouse can also appropriate and rearrange old bird nests like those of the magpie. The fat dormouse and the garden dormouse may make their summer nests in a wall, a heap of wood or a hollow tree. The winter nests where they hibernate are very different and are built underground or in deep holes sheltered from the cold.

The harvest mouse and the hazel dormouse build nests about 12 cm in diameter in the heart of dense vegetation, usually at a height of less than 2 m above the ground. That of the hazel dormouse is made of many materials and simply rests in the forks of vegetation whilst that of the harvest mouse is made of grass and strongly intertwined with the stems of the vegetation in which it shelters. The nests of these small mammals are most easily discovered in autumn when the leaves have fallen. Abandoned nests are then visible and further visits to the same sites the following summer should help to find new nests plus their occupants.

BUILDINGS

Of the European mammals only the beaver and the muskrat make structures to live in. Sometimes these species live in burrows but if the habitat is favourable they can build very impressive structures.

The muskrat, originally from North America, resists the rigours of winter in an original and efficaceous way. Each autumn it builds at the edge of a body of water, heaps of vegetation collected in the area – plants, branches and leaves plus mud. The diameter at the base of these buildings is about 1–2 m and the height up to 0.5–1.5 m. The entrance and the tunnels are below water and lead to a chamber in the heart of the mass of vegetation which serves as insulation and not food.

The beaver is the only true builder in Europe but is much more discreet than the muskrat. The persecution of the beaver and the disturbance of its building sites have made this animal live more in tunnels. In France and Scandinavia, there is legislation protecting the beaver and it has once again begun to build structures – mostly dams and heaps of vegetation.

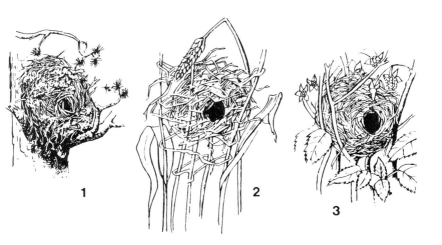

Like birds some mammals build aerial nests: 1 squirrel; 2 harvest mouse; 3 hazel dormouse.

Use of Observations and Preservation of Traces

The field notebook

The use of a field notebook is indispensable to the study of mammals. No guide book can replace carefully recorded personal experience and no publication, however detailed, can record all the observations

Section of a muskrat hut which can measure 1.50 m in diameter and may reach a height of 1 m.

noted in the course of years of study. As time goes on the field notes become even more important. Each partial observation made on a single day is supplemented by another later, and only the field notebook allows the combination of the accumulated observations. It is wise to change field notebooks regularly, at least every six months; this will avoid too great a loss of information if the book is mislaid during work in the field.

Many events in the lives of mammals take place at defined seasons. A short break of two or three weeks in field work will often leave a gap which cannot be filled until the following year. Well kept field notes over several years help the observer to predict, for example, the date of emergence of young badgers, and ensure that the event is not missed.

One of the best times to see otters is the period when frogs and toads gather in large numbers in ponds to reproduce. For about 15 days, at the end of March and beginning of April, the otters arrive each night

The beaver builds large heaps of vegetation.

to exploit this food supply. This is an occasion not to be missed and its timing should be carefully recorded.

If the event has been missed there is a second chance. The field notebook may record that the reproductive period of the amphibians is later at higher altitudes giving the observer another opportunity to see the otters. This indicates the importance of keeping careful note of important facts especially: place, date, weather, and all events that might change the appearance of traces or the behaviour of the animal.

To avoid the enormous task of having to compile a great quantity of information scattered through several notebooks it is easier to assemble the notes from time to time by species and by theme – this is also the easiest way to collate ones knowledge.

Example from a page of a typical field notebook

Date   : 18 August 1988
Time   : 16.40
Species   : *Mus musculus*
Locality   : Tring, Hertfordshire
Habitat   : under woodpile in farmyard, close to barn
Observations : nest with tracks parallel to barn wall, two young, female escapes. Farmer reports damage to stored wheat.

Making casts of prints

No drawing or photograph can reproduce a print as well as a plaster cast. Apart from the pleasure gained from the activity, making a collection of plaster casts is the best way to study the tracks of animals in three dimensions. Plaster casts also allow comparison between prints. Some people use wax to make casts but plaster, which has the advantage of being poured cold, is much easier to use. The materials are very simple: a small bag of rapid setting plaster, an old jar and a bottle of water and some moulds, rectangular or round.

Evenly shaped wooden moulds have the advantage of producing casts that are easy to store in drawers or boxes without waste of space, but they may be heavy, cumbersome, easily broken and difficult to make. The best moulds are plastic tubing of different diameters (3–15 cm). It is neccessary to take care to cut the tubes cleanly at the top or the plaster will be difficult to remove.

Water and plaster are mixed, in equal parts, and the liquid gently poured into the mould surrounding the print so that the important details are not damaged.

In good weather and temperature conditions the mould may be removed in about half an hour. After making sure that the plaster is really dry, it can be cleaned using a soft brush under a tap or in a stream. The result is a negative image in three dimensions. To obtain an exact copy of the original print (the positive) a second mould can be made, by the same method, covering the negative with vaseline or detergent to avoid the two parts sticking together.

The preservation and analysis of droppings

The study of the traces left by animals is one thing, to know how to share the knowledge is another. To reach this objective it is necessary to make original collections, notably of droppings. It is important to emphasise the problems of disease already mentioned. It is very important to avoid handling the droppings of animals especially those of carnivores. After collection it is necessary to allow them to dry and to, label each sample correctly with species, date and locality.

If the collection is made in order to study the diet of a species, treatment of the droppings varies according to the species. The faeces of carnivores should be allowed to dry in the open air before dissecting and examining the contents for bits of bone, hairs or feathers, pieces of vegetation or invertebrates. The use of a binocular microscope is necessary for the smaller parts such as the bristle of worms often eaten by badgers and foxes.

If you are studying the diet of small herbivores (rodents or lagomorphs) it is neccessary to use a different technique and to macerate the droppings in a solution of sodium hypochlorite. Look for pieces of undigested vegetation that can be compared with reference material taken from the area and identified.

The insectivores (hedgehogs, shrews and bats) produce a very dry guano made up of fine debris of insects – pieces of leg, wing and antennae. Here too a reference collection is indispensable for identifying the material.

A REFERENCE COLLECTION OF BONY REMAINS

Natural history museums keep large collections of reference material. However these are not always available when a bone or a skull needs identifying. It might be possible to identify the material at a local museum or even to make your own collection. The second solution has advantages but there are some difficulties. For example it is difficult to obtain permission to collect protected species. Remember that a permit may be needed to pick up a dead bat at the side of the road.

If the remains of a small rodent or a shrew are found by the roadside it is useful to preserve the skull and the long bones after identification. The simplest procedure is to macerate the head in water and progressively remove the loose pieces of flesh. At the end of the operation hydrogen peroxide may be used to bleach the specimen (boiling the head of some mammals such as rodents and shrews may damage the fragile structure but this technique can be used for more robust material).

Collecting specimens of skulls and bones of small mammals is very useful for the identification of the remains from rejection pellets of birds of prey and from the droppings of carnivores.

REFERENCE COLLECTION OF OTHER TRACES

Observers are seldom sufficiently curious. There are quantities of small traces seen but not collected or which are noted in an imprecise fashion because they are regarded as of little importance but may actually constitute an important source of data about the species being studied. Do not hesitate to collect, along with the plaster casts of tracks, the remains of meals, traces of activity (nuts, pine cones, cut branches, etc) plus any other indicators.

As soon as one starts collecting specimens, it is important to determine the place where they are to be stored, to evaluate the time taken

The clarity of this fox print is suitable for making a useful plaster cast.

The coypu cuts stems to reach the seeds.

to identify them and to think about the use to which they can be put. A museum or the collection of a society are perhaps the best places to keep such a collection making it available to other students, because there is little doubt that such a collection will be consulted by many.

THE PROTECTION OF MAMMALS AND RECENT STUDIES

With human pressure becoming ever greater, the living space for mammals is further reduced as each year passes. Some species have been eradicated from the whole continent, including Great Britain, others are threatened with disappearance from certain countries. Studies made by enthusiastic amateurs and professional scientists have increased our knowledge of mammals, bringing to light the dangers facing them and helping to plan measures for their rescue, protection and intelligent reintroduction. Such studies may also help to explain fluctuations about which there are still unsolved problems.

THE ROLE OF AMATEURS AND THE IMPORTANCE OF FIELD WORK

The regular presence of mammalogists in the field is indispensable, not only to obtain results, but also to appreciate the pressures affecting the animals and their habitats.

THREATENED SPECIES

To study mammals is one thing, to actively work for the protection of species and habitats is another. In Europe some species are effectively protected but the habitats where they live receive less attention. Without habitat conservation the animals have no chance of survival. This is the case for the brown bear in France where there is no habitat left.

International agreements concerning the protection of animals depend principally on two conventions:

n otter spraint full of toad bones.   *The otter, one of the rarer species and difficult to watch.*

Convention of International Trade and Endangered Species of Wild Fauna and Flora (CITES)

Convention on the Conservation of European Wildlife and Natural Habitats (BERN).

In Europe (and this includes Great Britain and Ireland) animals are protected by a number of laws and regulations and anyone interested in studying wildlife should be familiar with them. Each country has its own legislation to protect species within its boundaries and it is not possible to list them all in this book. The principal European legislation is included in the following publications:

European Council Regulation 3626/82 (as amended)

European Commission Regulations 3418/83

European Council Directive 79/409/EEC
European Commission Directive 85/411/EEC
In Great Britain the two most important documents, which in many ways go beyond the internationally agreed conventions, are:
Endangered Species (Import and Export) Act 1976 (UK)
Wildlife and Countryside Act 1981 (UK)

SAFEGUARDS AND ACTIVE PROTECTION

The question has often been posed – Why protect? But how can we justify the extinction of a species? The problem is no longer a scientific, economic or emotional problem, it is in the realm of morals and ethics. If it is true that an animal, by its existence, can provide interesting scientific information or be a source of economic value this is of secondary importance by comparison with the survival of the species.

In this context the action of protection has several goals. The fashion for reintroductions has now become popular. Some successes are undeniable (the ibex in the Alps), others remain unproven.

It is a grave error to assume that the elimination of species is not important because in some cases replacement is possible. Even successful reintroductions can prejudice the less well publicised work of protection and the constant surveillance of still existing populations. It seems paradoxical to envisage the reintroduction of the brown bear in the Alps if we are incapable of stopping the disappearance of the same species still living in other areas.

INTRODUCTION OF SPECIES AND THE CONSEQUENCES

For thousands of years man has taken animals on his voyages. It is by this means that the fallow deer and the mouflon reached Europe. More recently the American mink, the muskrat, the racoon, and possibly the racoon dog have enriched the fauna through human action.

However, the practical problems of introducing exotic species are poorly understood. There are also ethical problems. Why should we mix faunas? Why not accept them as they are? The work of biogeographers will become impossible if all faunas are disturbed.

It is also neccessary to consider the economic effects, the health and the genetic aspects of these introductions which are impossible to measure in advance (particularly as the necessary studies are seldom even tried).

Reason and experience suggests that introductions should be attempted only with extreme caution.

FLUCTUATIONS

In some species of voles *(Microtus* and *Arvicola)* there are periodic peaks of populations which occur every three or four years and are of variable intensity. They are not synchronous between species nor in different regions. It is astonishing how quickly some species can take advantage of favourable conditions. It may be that modern agricultural practices play a part in the phenomenon and these have become so modified that they are perhaps difficult to reverse. The consequences of these fluctuations are serious. Instead of bringing into question some of our agricultural practices it is more usual to treat the area with massive doses of rodenticides thus endangering a wide spectrum of our remaining wildlife.

– THE MAMMALS –

THE WESTERN HEDGEHOG
Erinaceus europaeus

FAMILY ERINACEIDAE

ECOLOGY AND BIOLOGY

Distribution The western hedgehog inhabits western Europe from southern Scandinavia and Finland, as well as the near Baltic states, through to the larger Mediterranean islands. It is the only species of hedgehog found in Britain and Ireland, where its distribution is widespread.

Description Total length 20–30 cm, of which 2–3.5 cm are tail; height to shoulder 12–15 cm; weight 0.4–1.4 kg (the male is heavier than the female).

With its spiny covering and its general appearance, the hedgehog cannot be confused with any other species. Its pointed head ends in a muzzle, the extremity of which is darker than the rest of the body. The mass of bicoloured spines 2–3 cm long protect its back and sides. The underside and face are covered with relatively soft light brown hair. Forepaws short and hindfeet have 5 digits armed with claws. The tail is hardly visible.

> **Similar species** *The eastern hedgehog and the Algerian hedgehog.*

Habitat and territory The hedgehog inhabits practically the whole of the temperate region. It can be found in deciduous woodland, grasslands, meadows, gardens and particularly on farmland. On mountains it is present at more than 1600 m but reproductive populations do not appear to be maintained at more than 1200 m.

Each individual seems to have its own territory which may vary between 4 and 40 ha in size depending on the amount of food available. The hedgehog prefers open areas to seek its food but during the winter months needs a well protected shelter – dense bushes, rabbit holes, compost heaps in gardens, barns in mountains in which to hibernate.

Food The hedgehog feeds mainly on a diet of insects, worms and slugs but it will also show opportunism. It can profit from explosions of insects in spring, fruits in summer and autumn, and, may also eat small vertebrates, which it has surprised, and carrion found along the roads.

Reproduction The breeding season begins soon after hibernation has ended. The male becomes sexually active a month before the female. This is why early couplings are often unsuccessful before mid–April. Gestation is about 40 days with the first litter appearing in late May. Each litter usually contains 4–5 young, which are naked and blind but soon acquire the first coat of white spines which are later replaced by normal spines. A series of long white hairs appears before the true spines. The female is receptive again in July and can produce a second litter during the summer.

◀ *The hedgehog.*

TRACES AND OBSERVATION

Indications of presence

NEST: although the hedgehog does not dig a hole, it does build a nest, which it lines with vegetation, to hibernate in during the winter.

TRACKS: the paws have 5 digits which leave easily recognised tracks in suitable soil. The forefoot is almost as broad as long (2.5 x 2.8 cm) while the hindfoot is more elongated (3 x 2 cm).

DROPPINGS: measuring 2–4 cm long by 1 cm diameter, they are left at random during movement. They are usually composed of the remains of insects (pieces of cuticle and elytra) unless the meal has been a vertebrate when the droppings will contain bits of bones. The droppings are very characteristic – regular and cylindrical.

> **Risks of confusion** *The tracks left by a hedgehog are similar to those of a brown rat or of a large vole (although these are smaller and have 4 digits on the forefeet).*

1 The western hedgehog
2 The eastern hedgehog

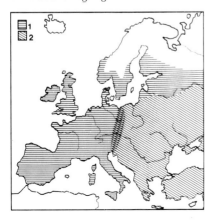

Observation Essentialy nocturnal, the hedgehog can be found on mild nights from March to November. The diversity of sites where they can be seen is enormous. The animal, always noisy, accompanies its movements with a continuous whistling while hunting for food. When disturbed it is capable of fleeing quickly and silently. In gardens one can attract them by offering food every evening; canned dog or cat food is much appreciated.

Their bodies are seen often on the roads. Faced with danger the little animal always reacts in the same way, by rolling into a ball. Although efficacious against a predator this behaviour is catastrophic when crossing a busy road. More than 150000 are killed each year on French roads.

RELATED SPECIES

The eastern hedgehog
Erinaceus concolor

This species replaces the western hedgehog in eastern Europe from Poland in the north to Yugoslavia in the south. It is principally distinguished by its white throat. The two species have similar habits and can be found together in a band about 200 km wide.

The Algerian hedgehog
Erinaceus algirus

This species is only found in continental Europe. Originally from north Africa it was introduced to the Mediterranean coasts of Spain and France (eastern Pyrenees, Var). It is also present in the Balearic islands and some individuals have been seen in Charente-Maritime.

Smaller than the western hedgehog and rarely weighing more than 800 g

its body has lighter underparts and its ears are relatively large. It appears rather higher on its paws. On the forehead the spines resemble a haircut with a centre parting.

THE NORTHERN MOLE
Talpa europaea

FAMILY TALPIDAE

ECOLOGY AND BIOLOGY

Distribution Although present in the greater part of Europe, this species is absent from Ireland and seldom if ever found in Scandinavia, southern Spain, Italy, Greece and the Mediterranean islands.

Description Total length 14–20 cm of which the tail is 2–4 cm; weight 70–120 g (male larger than female).

This species is characterised by its cylindrical form, absence of neck, no external ears and the extremely small eyes hidden in the very short, soft black fur. The forefeet in the form of shovels that stick out to the side are perfectly adapted to its tunnelling habit.

> **Similar species** *The blind mole and the Roman mole.*

Habitat and territory Because of its subterranean activities, the mole shows a preference for soil which is easy to excavate, well drained, deep and not too dry. It can be found in grasslands and gardens, leafy forests,

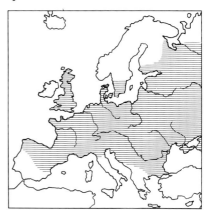

The European or Northern mole.

plains and mountains, where it is present up to 2000 m if there is sufficient depth of soil. Each individual tunnels its own system of galleries which can be as much as 200 m long. Mole hills are the waste which the animal ejects regularly to the surface, normally without any hole.

The forefoot of a mole.
1 dorsal   2 ventral

71

Food Earthworms and insect larvae form the basic diet. From time to time the mole will feed at the surface on small snails and slugs. On occasions it will store earthworms after first cutting the anterior segments to immobilise them.

Reproduction In moles the breeding season is short – usually April and May. At this time the males connect their tunnel systems with those of nearby females. It is the only time of year when cohabitation can be observed. The gestation period lasts for about 4 weeks. The young are born in a nest of vegetation always built in the base of a large molehill called the fortress. They become independent at around the age of 5 weeks and then go

The mole seldom emerges from its tunnels.

off to form their own territories. Young come to the surface more often then adults.

TRACES AND OBSERVATION

Indications of presence

NEST: molehills are indications of the underground presence of moles. It is important to distinguish them from

anthills (where the earth is much more compact and often covered in vegetation) and the small hills left by some voles (see water vole). The molehill is conical with the diameter at the base about 30 cm; when fresh the buttons of earth rejected by the mole can be clearly seen (see illustration).

SUPERFICIAL TUNNELS: most of the tunnels regularly dug by moles represent explorations which they make to seek food. Shallow, except in times of drought, the tunnels are sometimes so close to the surface that they can be seen, mainly in woodland, as a small straight ridge on the soil.

Risks of confusion The 'molehills' of the vole and the mole can easily be confused. As for those of the blind mole and the Roman mole, it is practically impossible to distinguish them from the European mole, but the areas of distribution of these species do not overlap except in southern Europe.

Observation It is not easy to observe directly an animal like the mole, which lives almost exclusively underground. Its activity is revealed most immediately by the sudden appearance of a new molehill or reinforcement of an old one. The pattern of work, during the day and night, is marked by periods of activity and rest of about 3–4 hours. The mole stays active all year round. It swims well and this can be seen if the animal is crossing a stream or fleeing in front of a flood.

It is not unusual to find dead moles at the soil surface. Some will have been killed, but not eaten, by some small carnivore.

RELATED SPECIES

The blind mole
Talpa caeca

The blind or Mediterranean mole replaces the European mole in the south of the continent: Spain, Provence, northern Italy and the coast of Dalmatia down to Greece. It is a little smaller than its relative and its eyes are totally covered with skin.

The Roman mole
Talpa romana

The only mole present in southern Italy (also found in the Balkans), it is a little larger than the European mole

and as in the blind mole its eyes are completely covered by skin.

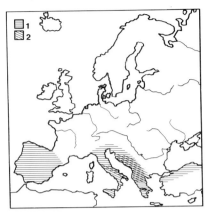

1 The blind mole
2 The Roman mole

The Pyrenean desman
Galemys pyrenaicus

FAMILY TALPIDAE

ECOLOGY AND BIOLOGY

Distribution The desman is confined to the French side of the Pyrenean chain and to the massifs of the northwest of the Iberian peninsula – Cantabrian mountains, Sierra de Gredos, Sierra de Guadarrama. In France there has been a reduction in the populations in the lowest parts of its range where it was once found at an altitude less than 400 m. Higher up, it can be found between 2500 and 3000 m.

Description Total length 24–28 cm, of which 11–13 cm are tail; weight 50–80 g.

The desman resembles a large shrew with the plumpness of a mole.

Its neck is hardly noticeable and its head ends in a small very mobile trumpet which is always moving. The forefeet are small although the hindfeet are well developed, and the strong palmate feet have digits armed with claws. The tail is almost as long as the combined head and body length. The fur is bicoloured – brown above and white below.

> **Similar species** *The water shrew, the water vole.*

Habitat and territory The desman lives in mountain torrents. It vacates those zones that have become disturbed by hydroelectric schemes or where the waters have become soiled by pollution. It is found in trout streams, in the mill races of old mills and even in mountain lakes.

The Pyrenean desman.

The desman seems to have territorial behaviour and perhaps defends a strip of water. Each individual lives a solitary life and systematically avoids its fellows. The length of bank forming its territory depends on the food available in the torrent.

Food Mountain torrents carry a mass of potential prey important for an insectivore. The quantity of food available is calculated to be about 50–60 kg per 24 hours for 100 m of stream. The prey that compose the staple diet of the desman are the larvae of aquatic insects, insects which fall into the water and crustaceans. Food is available all the year round and it searches tirelessly the bed of the stream, turning pebbles all the while swimming against the strong current.

Reproduction The breeding season begins in January for the desman, the amount of food available is at a maximum during the first half of the year and it lasts until July. The females will give birth to two litters, with four to

five young in each, during the season. The contact between males and females is certainly brief and there is no detailed information on the biology of this species. The gestation period is about four weeks, as is the growing period of the young.

TRACES AND OBSERVATION

Indications of presence Even specialists admit that not one of them has been able to observe the Pyrenean desman properly in its own habitat. However, trout fishermen have known it for a long time and see it occasionally on river banks, despite its nocturnal habits.

NEST: the desman does not use a family nest, only a natural hole in the bank or a gap between tree roots. It seems to be well adapted to cold.

TRACKS: it is virtually impossible to find tracks in the terrain.

DROPPINGS: small and twisted black and brilliant when moist. They are deposited systematically out of the water, on a stone sticking above water level and they are very difficult to find. They have a strong odour which plays a role in intraspecific olfactory signalling.

> **Risk of confusion** *Despite its large size, the desman, when found in the water resembles the water shrew. The fur of the two species appears silver when they dive because of the air retained amongst the hairs. However, the water shrew is much smaller. The aquatic rodents such as the water rat do not frequent the same mountain biotopes.*

Observation Certainly not easy. To hope to see a desman it is necessary to stand on a bridge over a stretch of a calm mountain stream, where the desman is known to live. And wait patiently...

THE ETRUSCAN SHREW
Suncus etruscus

<small>FAMILY SORICIDAE</small>

ECOLOGY AND BIOLOGY

Distribution In Europe the distribution of the Etruscan shrew (also known as the pygmy white-toothed shrew) is southerly – Spain and Italy. It is found on the Mediterranean islands and in France; the distribution follows that of the holm oak out to the Atlantic coast.

Description Total length 6–10 cm, of which 2.4–3 cm is tail; weight about 2 g.

The Etruscan shrew is the smallest European mammal. Mainly grey, its upper surface is lightly tinged with brown and long scattered hairs emerge from the fur and along the tail. This last character is common to all the white–toothed shrews. The ears are relatively large and the tail long.

1 The pygmy–toothed shrew.
2 The Pyrenean desman.

> **Similar species** *Young white–toothed shrews (*Crocidura *spp) can be confused with adult Etruscan shrews.*

Habitat and territory The Etruscan shrew seeks warm, exposed rocky habitats. Dry stone walls around vineyards provide an ideal habitat for this species enabling it to survive in areas north of its normal distribution.

Solitary, each individual actively defends its territory against its neighbours. Markers are olfactory (from lateral glands) and auditory (cries).

Food An insectivore, the Etruscan shrew attacks all invertebrates it encounters that are smaller in size than a cricket.

Reproduction Several litters may be born each season. Males and females stay together only long enough to breed. Gestation is estimated to be 27 days, the average number of young per litter is between three and six. At birth they weigh about as much as a coffee bean.

TRACES AND OBSERVATION

Indications of presence The population density of Etruscan shrews is never high and is generally lower than for the other shrews found in the same areas. To confirm their presence it is necessary to analyse the rejection pellets of birds of prey in the region (indirect index) or to systematically prospect the dry walls of cultivated terraces.

> ***Risks of confusion*** *The lesser white–toothed shrew and the North African mouse are found in the same habitats. Very quick observation of a fugitive small mammal is not always sufficient for identification.*

Observation Direct observation is difficult. The animal is active all the year round and does not seem to have a marked daily period of activity. Study in captivity remains one of the few ways to get to know this very small animal but to capture such a small and delicate creature alive is hard.

THE WATER SHREW
Neomys fodiens

FAMILY SORICIDAE

ECOLOGY AND BIOLOGY

Distribution The water shrew is found throughout Europe with the exception of Ireland, most of Spain, the Greek peninsula and the shores of the Black Sea. It is also absent from the Mediterranean islands.

Description Total length 12–15 cm of which 5–7 cm are tail; weight 8–24 g.

The water shrew is the largest of the European shrews. It is usually bicoloured – dark brown on the back and white below. It has a pointed muzzle as in all shrews. The points of the teeth are red. The eyes are small and the ears are hidden beneath very dense fur. The hind feet of the animal are fringed with a comb of long hairs to assist swimming. The tail is also bicoloured and has on the lower edge a comb of swimming hairs.

> **Similar species** *The rest of the shrews, in particular Miller's shrew,*

Habitat and territory The water shrew is found in a large number of habitats, usually close to water (rivers, lakes). It is also found in damp meadows but individuals have been trapped several kilometres from the nearest body of water. The water shrew is more semi–aquatic than truly aquatic. Some individuals are capable of living on shingle beaches above the tidal zone. On mountains they are present at more than 2000 m. Living on the banks of rivers, water shrews are solitary, each having its own territory. They dig tunnels in the banks with the help of their front feet and their noses.

Food The water shrew can hunt as well in water as it can on land. Prey captured in water (insect larvae, small fish, amphibians) are consumed on land. They seem to store food, accumulating the remains of partially consumed meals in specific places. On land they eat invertebrates.

Reproduction Individual territories are adjacent or slightly overlapping, males and females therefore meet without difficulty. The breeding season extends from April to September, each female giving birth to several litters during this period. They remain together for a short time; 3–8 young (maximum 11) are born after a gestation period of about 24 days.

TRACES AND OBSERVATION

Indications of presence Water shrews are difficult to see in the field. Most of the information on their biology has been gathered by observing the behaviour of captive specimens.

The water shrew seldom wanders far from water.

NEST: water shrews can re–use mole tunnels or will build their own. On the banks of water courses the nests are always difficult to find. The remains of partly consumed meals (fish, frogs) can give an indication of its presence.

PRINTS: at the edge of rivers when the waters fall after winter floods, small beaches of very fine grain silt sometimes appear, which may provide an opportunity for discovering the tracks of a shrew. Five digits on each foot may be seen. The tail of the animal may also leave a faint trail on the ground between the footprints. If this tiny track leads to the water one can conclude that it is a water shrew.

> ***Risks of confusion*** *Tracks of a similar type are left by Miller's shrews. The hole of the water shrew must be distinguished from those of the water vole. The prints resemble those of aquatic rodents (water vole, brown rat) but in these cases the fingers of the forefeet are much larger.*

Observation It is easier to discover a dead water shrew than to see one living. The animal is active all the year round, day and night, alternating rest and activity. If one waits patiently near a river bank where they are known to live one can usually see the animal as a small silver ball which seems to work hard to stay at the bottom of the water; as soon as it stops swimming it rises to the surface like a bubble.

RELATED SPECIES

Miller's water shrew
Neomys anomalus

This shrew is very similar to the water shrew. It is however a little smaller and has fewer swimming hairs. Its distribution in Europe is limited to mountainous regions.

1 The water shrew.
2 Miller's water shrew.

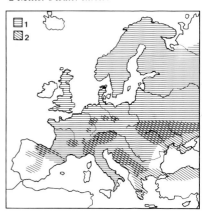

THE COMMON SHREW AND MILLET'S SHREW
Sorex araneus and *Sorex coronatus*

FAMILY SORICIDAE

ECOLOGY AND BIOLOGY

Distribution It has been recently shown that more than one species of shrew is included under the name common shrew. In fact the common shrew is found at altitude in the Alps, Pyrenees and Massif Central, but in the plains of Alsace, Ailleurs in France, it is replaced by Millet's shrew. In Europe, Millet's shrew is found only on the North Atlantic coast of Spain and parts of France, whilst the common shrew is found in Britain, but not Ireland, and over most of the continent of Europe.

Description Total length 8–12 cm of which 3–4.5 cm are tail; weight 5–13 g.

The common shrew is slightly larger than Millet's shrew. The two species are almost identical in appearance and are difficult to distinguish when they occupy the same area. These species can be identified by examination of the chromosomes. In the field careful data on the location gives a good indication.

The common shrew represents the type for the family with the characteristic pointed mobile snout. The eyes are small and almost invisible and the ears partially hidden in the short, dense, velvety fur. The pelage is dark brown above though the flanks are lighter and the underside has a shade of yellow. The points of the teeth are dark red. As with other shrews each foot has five digits with claws.

Similar species *Pygmy shrew and other crocidurine shrews.*

Habitat and territory The common shrew and Millet's shrew have many points in common. The common shrew is found in all types of habitat throughout Europe from mountains at altitudes over 1000 m to plains in the swampy regions of Alsace and Lorraine. It is better adapted to the cold than its relative which prefers the temperate oceanic climate. Both can be found in most habitats except the driest areas. A cover of dense vegetation at soil level is favourable. These two shrews are capable of burrowing in soft soil with the aid of nose and forefeet, passing a large part of the winter in underground shelters.

Food Insectivorous and carnivorous, these shrews eat all types of small invertebrates present in the soil litter. They also consume the corpses of small vertebrates and make food stores.

Reproduction Both species can reproduce throughout the year. After a gestation period of about 20 days the shrew give birth to 4–10 young. Each female can have four to six litters in one season.

TRACES AND OBSERVATION

Indications of presence The occurrence of these shrews in an area is usually detected by the presence of their corpses on the ground. It may be an individual killed by a small carnivore or an animal having died of old age – at the end of its second summer season. Presence can also be detected by examining the rejection pellets of nocturnal birds of prey in which the bony remains of the animals can be found. In fact, contrary to what happens with carnivores birds of prey do actually eat the shrews.

In addition it is possible to hear the sharp aggressive cries coming from thick grass or from under the litter in a forest, which may be due to an agressive encounter between two animals or an attempt at coupling.

> ***Risks of confusion*** *All traces left by other species of shrew.*

Observation Although widespread and active both by day and night

shrews remain difficult to track in the field. From time to time they are caught by domestic cats. If the shrew is still alive and regains its freedom it can be seen fleeing in a jerky and hesitant manner, feeling its way with its nose and whiskers. Shrews can be easily caught in traps (but this is illegal in some countries). In this way they can be easily studied. However, it is necessary to examine the traps frequently and not to keep them too long as they are very fragile and must eat frequently as they need to eat about their own body weight of food each day.

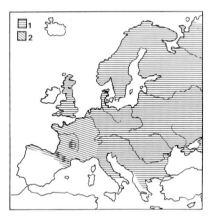

1 The common shrew.
2 Millet's shrew.

THE PYGMY SHREW
Sorex minutus

FAMILY SORICIDAE

ECOLOGY AND BIOLOGY

Distribution This small shrew is found almost throughout Europe with the exception of the Mediterranean islands. It is the only shrew found in Ireland.

Description Total length 7–11 cm, of which 3–4.6 cm are tail; weight 2.5–7 g.

The pygmy shrew resembles a small common shrew. The pelage is

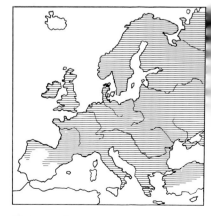

The pygmy shrew.

bicoloured: grey-brown above and clear grey below. The tail is relatively long and can exceed two–thirds of the body length. The teeth are red coloured.

> **Similar species** *The common shrew and Millet's shrew.*

Habitat and territory The pygmy shrew inhabits the same areas as the common and Millet's shrews but prefers the more humid regions with dense vegetation. It is sensitive to dryness and is only present at altitude in the Mediterranean region. It lives on the surface, in the litter, particularly in winter when the Millet's shrew is in its underground shelter.

Food and reproduction The pygmy shrew feeds on the small invertebrates that are present in the litter. The breeding pattern is similar to that of Millet's shrew but with a shorter breeding season.

FOOD AND OBSERVATION

Observation Indications of its presence are similar to those for Millet's shrew but the pygmy shrew is even more difficult to find as it has a much lower population density.

THE ALPINE SHREW
Sorex alpinus

FAMILY SORICIDAE

ECOLOGY AND BIOLOGY

Distribution The alpine shrew lives in the mountain massifs of Europe – the Alps, Jura, Harz and Tatra mountains.

Description Total length 12–15 cm of which 6–8 cm are tail; weight 6–10 g.
  This shrew is easy to identify; its coat is grey–black and the tail is as long as the head and body. The ears do not appear above the fur and the points of the teeth are dark red.

Habitat and territory Although associated with mountains, living at altitudes exceeding 2000 m, the alpine

The alpine shrew.

shrew can be found in lowlands of central Europe at less than 300 m. It is an animal of rocky habitats, frequenting the stony banks of mountain streams.

Food and reproduction It eats mostly small invertebrates. The only difference in reproduction from the other shrews is that the breeding season begins later, having two or three litters between the end of spring and the start of autumn.

Observation Precise information on this species is lacking. Although its habitat is well known it usually escapes observation. Living amongst and in the cracks of rocks, it seems well adapted to jumping between the stones (a sight not often seen).

THE COMMON WHITE–TOOTHED SHREW
Crocidura russula

FAMILY SORICIDAE

ECOLOGY AND BIOLOGY

Distribution The common white–toothed shrew is found in the western part of Europe, but is absent from Italy, Corsica and the British mainland (although present on the Channel Islands).

Description Total length 10–14 cm, of which 3–5 cm is tail; weight 6–15 g.

The largest of the white–toothed shrews, it has a grey pelage, lightly tinged with brown on the upper side, lighter below but without a clear demarcation. Ears are clearly visible and long sparse hairs emerge from the fine covering of the tail. The teeth are white. These last three characters are common to the three species of *Crocidura*.

> **Similar species** *Bicoloured white–toothed shrew and lesser white–toothed shrew.*

Food Like most other white–toothed shrews, this species feeds mostly on small invertebrates but also occasionally eats the corpses of small vertebrates.

Reproduction The breeding season can extend for about six months – from spring to the end of summer. Several litters, averaging three or four young, maximum ten, are born during

1 *The bicoloured white–toothed shrew.*
2 *The common white–toothed shrew.*

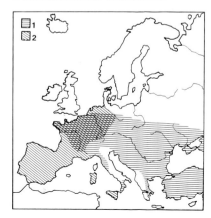

the season. The gestation period is about 30 days. The nest, composed of leaves, moss and blades of dry grasses, is often built in the heart of a tuft of vegetation, at the base of a bush or under a stone.

Habitat and territory The white–toothed shrew is well adapted to the Mediterranean countryside – forests of cork–oak, bush and dry stone walls. It seeks a protective cover of vegetation – hedges, bushes, sparse grass. In the northern part of its distribution it is found mostly in very dry habitats, and on mountains, its range includes altitudes of more than 1500 m. This shrew frequently lives close to houses and even enters towns.

OBSERVATION

Observation In most places the white–toothed shrew is very difficult to observe either directly or indirectly. The remains of skulls in the rejection pellets of birds of prey are a good indication of its presence and road casualties are often found. The difficulties in observation of the other white–toothed shrews are true also for this species. Nevertheless its colour, dominantly grey, its liveliness and its abundance make it one of the shrews that one has the best chance of seeing.

THE BICOLOURED WHITE–TOOTHED SHREW
Crocidura leucodon

FAMILY SORICIDAE

ECOLOGY AND BIOLOGY

Distribution The bicoloured white–toothed shrew is found throughout central Europe from Brittany to the Black Sea. It is absent from the British Isles, northern Europe, the Iberian peninsula, the south–west quarter of France and Corsica.

Description Total length 9–13 cm of which 3–4 cm are tail; weight 7–14 g.

A little smaller than the common white–toothed shrew and with a slightly shorter tail. Pelage bicoloured, very dark above and almost white below with a clear line of demarcation. Thus

easy to distinguish from the other white toothed shrews.

> **Similar species** *Common and lesser white–toothed shrews.*

Habitat and territory The bicoloured white–toothed shrew is less widespread than the common white–toothed shrew and is in fact poorly known. It frequents covered and rather wet areas and has been found on mountains up to 1000 m.

Food and reproduction It feeds mostly on small invertebrates. Poorly known, the reproduction of this species may be similar to that of related species.

OBSERVATION

Observation Traces of this species are not easy to find, partly because of its relative rarity. A study of the bones (particularly skulls) in the rejection pellets of nocturnal birds of prey is important in this species. Although it is active day and night all the year round, this species is more difficult to find than the other shrews.

The common white—toothed shrew.

THE LESSER WHITE–TOOTHED SHREW
Crocidura suaveolens

FAMILY SORICIDAE

ECOLOGY AND BIOLOGY

Distribution Of the three species of white–toothed shrews found in Europe this is the most Mediterranean. It is found in the north and west of Spain, in Portugal, in Italy and in the east as far as the Black Sea. It is also present in Corsica and on the Mediterranean isles but is absent from most of northern Europe including Scandinavia, Ireland and mainland Britain, although it does occur on some Scilly and Channel Islands.

Description Total length 8–12 cm of which 3–4.5 cm are tail; weight 3–6 g.

In Corsica individuals are noticeably larger and weigh 10–13 g. Similar to the larger common white–toothed shrew, with a grey–brown pelage above and lighter below without clear demarcation. The ears are visible. In the final analysis examination of the teeth helps to distinguish the species.

> **Similar species** Pygmy white–toothed shrew and young specimens of the common white–toothed shrew.

The lesser white-toothed shrew.

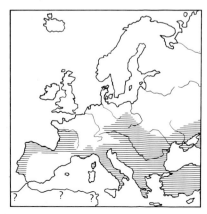

Habitat and territory The lesser white–toothed shrew prefers warm places and approaches areas of human habitation. In fact it can be found in many varied habitats.

Food and reproduction It feeds mainly on small invertebrates. Reproduction is probably comparable to that of the common white–toothed shrew.

Observation This species leaves fewer traces of its presence than other shrews. Again examination of rejection pellets of birds of prey can be rewarding. To find the animal in its habitat is usually a matter of luck.

CHIROPTERA

EUROPEAN FREE-TAILED BAT
Tadarida teniotis

FAMILY MOLOSSIDAE

ECOLOGY AND BIOLOGY

Distribution A Mediterranean species, this bat is found in riverine regions of Europe; the most northerly limit to its range is the Rhone river valley in Switzerland and France.

Description Total length 12.5–14.5 cm of which 4.5–5.5 cm are tail; forearm 57–64 mm; wingspan 40 cm; weight 25–30 g.

The free–tailed bat has a characteristic appearance – ears turned forwards and wrinkled muzzle. Its tail, the end of which is free from the membrane, is typical of the Family.

Habitat and territory A cliff–dwelling bat. This species prefers stony places and is often found flattened into a fissure. It can also be found in large buildings and in between the stone joints of bridges.

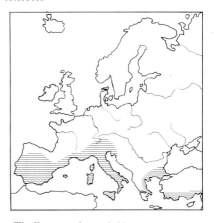

The European free-tailed bat.

Food and reproduction The free–tailed bat hunts high in the sky feeding on large insects. The females form small reproductive colonies.

TRACES AND OBSERVATION

Indications of presence This bat usually occupies inaccessible places and is difficult to discover, especially as the species is not very gregarious. It has a characteristic flight pattern.

Risks of confusion *Because of its large size and distinctive habitat, diagnosis is easily made.*

Observation The free–tailed bat emerges early in the evening, as do the swallows and martins. Its flight is straight and does not include rapid changes of direction. The animal emits strong, sharp cries, audible at a distance. It hunts in groups, with open mouth. The tail may be visible in flight.

The greater horseshoe bat.

THE GREATER HORSESHOE BAT
Rhinolophus ferrumequinum

Family Rhinolophidae

ECOLOGY AND BIOLOGY

Distribution The greater horseshoe bat still inhabits a large part of Europe but has a more southerly range than the lesser horseshoe bat. It is absent from Ireland and in Britain it is confined to the west of England and to the south of Wales. It is still found in various places in France but its numbers are reduced. In fact the species is declining. It is estimated, for example, that the population in Great Britain is only two per cent of that present in 1900.

Description Total length 8.5–11 cm of which 3–4 cm are tail; length of

forearm 50–61 mm, wingspan 35–40 cm; weight 16–34 g.

It is the largest European rhinolophine, having thick fur which is grey–brown above and whitish below. The nose leaf is characteristic.

Similar species *All other rhinolphines.*

Habitat and territory The greater horseshoe bat is associated with wooded areas that are interspersed with clearings and is usually found near water. The roost in summer is often in buildings, whereas in winter it is somewhere subterranean and damp, for example caves, grottos and mines.

Food and reproduction These bats feed mainly on night-flying moths, but they will also eat beetles. Reproduction is similar to the lesser horseshoe bat. The segregation of the sexes in summer is particularly marked.

TRACES AND OBSERVATION

Indications of presence As these bats hang hooked on by their feet and are enveloped in their wings they are easy to find in their roosts. The presence of guano (droppings) gives a good indication of their presence.

Observation Frequently seen in cultivated areas. The greater horseshoe bat has a large broad silhouette and emerges late in the evening. Their flight is relatively slow and low along hedges and embankments, and the wingbeats alternate with short gliding phases.

Some colonies are inhabited all year round. In winter it seems they change roosts easily for no known reason. They are very sensitive to disturbance.

1 Mehely's horseshoe bat.
2 Blasius' horseshoe bat.

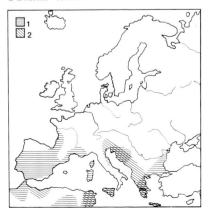

RELATED SPECIES

Mehely's horseshoe bat
Rhinolophus mehelyi

Mainly a Mediterranean species. Intermediate in size between the greater and lesser horseshoes, this species seems to have disappeared recently from France, possibly due to hunting by collectors of rare species. Little is known about its biology.

Blasius' horseshoe bat
Rhinolophus blasii

In Europe it is found around the Adriatic sea and in Sicily, Bulgaria and Crete. A little smaller than the above species. Characteristic nose leaf design.

The Mediterranean (Euryaline) horseshoe bat
Rhinolophus euryale

A circum–Mediterranean species. Found in the southern half of France, it resembles Mehely's horseshoe bat. Pelage is lighter than that of the

The Mediterranean horseshoe bat.

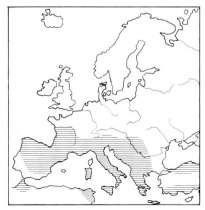

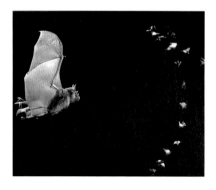

greater or lesser horseshoe bats. It seems to prefer relatively wooded areas and roosts in underground shelters (caves, mines). When at rest it is covered by its wings with only the nose leaf remaining apparent. This is the most gregarious of the horseshoe bats. The population appears to be declining and is becoming rare, especially in France.

The greater horseshoe bat hunting.

THE LESSER HORSESHOE BAT
Rhinolophus hipposideros

FAMILY RHINOLOPHIDAE

ECOLOGY AND BIOLOGY

Distribution Of all the European rhinolophs this is the most widely distributed and the most northerly. It is present from the western coast of Ireland and southern Great Britain to the Black Sea. However its population appears to be in major decline and it has already disappeared from parts of Germany and the Low Countries. It can still be found occasionally in France and Corsica.

The decline in numbers of the species seems to be general throughout Europe. A satisfactory explanation has not yet been found but it is no doubt the result of several factors such as modification of the habitat by humans, general use of chemical pesticides and ecological changes.

Description Total length 6–8 cm of which 2.5–3 cm are tail; length of

forearm 35–42 mm; wingspan 19–25 cm; weight 4–10 g.

All the rhinolophs have a characteristic nose leaf, each species having a particular design, which must be examined from the front and side for a positive identification. The ears of the lesser horseshoe bat are well developed, pointed at the tip but almost without tragus. They are very mobile when the animal is active. The fur is grey–brown, lighter below.

> **Similar species** *All other rhinolophs.*

Habitat and territory The lesser horseshoe bat is a cavernicolous species, found up to altitudes of 2000 m in the Alps. It lives in the grottos and caves, and in the roofs of houses. It often nests close to human habitation and can be found hunting in parks, gardens and wooded areas. It seems to stay close to its winter retreat, even in summer. The animal can pass the winter in the cellar of a house, moving to the roof space in summer. This species has been found in burrows. They hibernate alone or in small scattered groups and in the summer the females gather together in colonies while the males remain more solitary.

Food The lesser horseshoe eats small insects caught in flight between two and five metres above ground. It rarely hunts above ten metres.

Reproduction In the lesser horseshoe bat mating takes place during the autumn (and perhaps also in spring, at the end of hibernation). Conception takes place in spring and the gestation period is about 10 weeks. One or two young are born about June. The female has two pectoral teats, as in all bats, although the rhinolophine bats also have two false teats situated near the genital orifice. The young, which are carried by the female during the

first few weeks of life, grip the false teats freeing the females' pectoral muscles for flight.

TRACES AND OBSERVATION

Indications of presence

NEST: the lesser horseshoe bat finds shelter in caves, attics of houses, stone buildings, mines, natural crevices or even in the dens of foxes or badgers.

DROPPINGS: because these bats rest in the roofs of their shelters hanging upside down, the discovery of the guano leads to the discovery of the bats themselves. If bats are absent from the place where guano is found they could be lesser horseshoes if, for example, the droppings are concentrated under the ridge of a roof. But it is not easy to distinguish between the the droppings of the greater and lesser horseshoe bats. Measuring 5–6 cm

The greater mouse—eared bat.

each dropping is cylindrical or oval. Use of guano alone as a character to identify the bats is insufficient.

Observation The lesser horseshoe is easy to see as it lives near human habitation and even inside houses. The bat is a sensitive animal. If a reproductive colony is found, great care must be taken not to disturb the bats which may leave the colony and in the process leave behind many of the young. In winter these bats are easy to

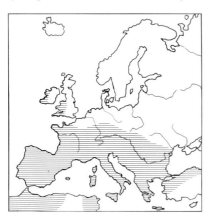

recognise, hooked to the roof of their colony, wrapped in their wings. The individuals can be alone or grouped but seldom touching each other. The roof where they are suspended is usually lower than that used by the greater horseshoe bat, but like the latter the lesser horseshoe bat seeks cool damp places. The resting position in winter is comparable to that in summer but the wings are not closed. The nose leaf is visible and identification is made easier. Sometimes the animals die suspended and may remain in this position for a long time.

In flight, the shape of this rhinoloph is somewhat heavy. It has broad wings and a heavy butterfly–like flight. It stops frequently while hunting above grass in a field or to explore foliage.

The lesser horseshoe bat.

THE GREATER MOUSE–EARED BAT
Myotis myotis

FAMILY VESPERTILIONIDAE

ECOLOGY AND BIOLOGY

Distribution This species is widespread in Europe except in the most northerly countries of Scandanavia including Denmark. It has, however, virtually disappeared from Great Britain and its numbers are steadily declining all over Europe. Since the end of the 1950s some colonies have disappeared and others have diminished by 80 per cent without clear reason – pesticides, disturbance, destruction of roosts, increase in human activity ...?

Description Total length 11–14 cm of which 4.5–6 cm are tail. Forearm 53–68 mm wingspan 35–45 cm; weight 20–40 g.

This is a large bat with well developed ears. The tragus is narrow throughout its length. The eyes are cleary visible and the pelage is brown above and whitish below. The greater mouse–eared bat is a 'typical' *Myotis*.

> **Similar species** *The lesser mouse–eared bat.*

Habitat and territory The greater mouse eared bat inhabits parks and gardens up to the edges of towns and fields bordered by patches of trees. To roost in summer it prefers large warm attics whilst in winter, caves and underground tunnels. The summer and winter roosts are often 100–200km apart. In summer the females gather in colonies whilst the males, more solitary, roost in hollow trees. The bat hibernates in mixed colonies with other bat species.

Food This bat specialises in hunting large terrestrial insects. It flies close to the ground catching beetles or grasshoppers. It also feeds on cockchafers. A capture of a shrew has been reported although this is exceptional.

Reproduction The reproductive strategy of the greater mouse–eared bat is similar to many other species of European bat. Mating takes place in autumn and fertilisation in spring. Births occur in June after a gestation period of 60–70 days. A single young is born.

TRACES AND OBSERVATION

Indications of presence In summer a colony of 100 bats roosting in a house becomes obvious because of the guano and the daily activity of the group. Males have a low pitched call similar to a buzz.

ROOST: in summer, in the northern part of the distribution the greater mouse–eared bat prefers large warm lofts of chateaux or large buildings. In the south, the winter roosts are subterranean.

DROPPINGS: analysis of the contents of the guano confirms that the insect remains are predominantly those of terrestrial species. Each dropping measures 1–1.5 cm long and consists of the chitin of insect skeletons which may give them a shiny appearance.

Observation Summer colonies are larger than the winter roosts. In warm weather this species can be found in attics which are both large and warm.

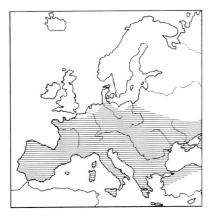

The greater mouse–eared bat.

Again it is important not to disturb the animals. In winter the individuals are suspended along a wall, remaining visible and not hiding in cracks. In flight the greater mouse–eared bat gives the impression of power with its rather slow rhythm of wingbeats. It emerges at nightfall and members of the colony follow each other in single file. They fly at about 30 m above ground to reach the hunting grounds. Here they can be seen prospecting the forest paths at ground level, along hedges and even landing to capture and devour a beetle or a grasshopper. The bats do not emerge in bad weather.

DAUBENTON'S BAT
Myotis daubentoni

FAMILY VESPERTILIONIDAE

ECOLOGY AND BIOLOGY

Distribution Daubenton's bat is found throughout Europe except in the north of Scandinavia and it is rare in the Balkan peninsula.

Description Total length 7–9.5 cm of which 3–4 cm are tail; length of forearm 33–42 mm; wingspan 21–25 cm; weight 5.5–15 g.
  A small species of bat, the pelage is brown above and clear grey on the belly, the muzzle is lightly tinged with red, and the bat is recognised essentially by the large feet.

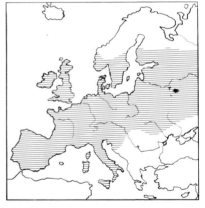

Daubenton's bat.

> **Similar species** *The long–fingered bat, the pond bat and other small* Myotis *spp.*

Habitat and territory Linked to areas of water, the Daubenton's bat seeks roosts in vegetation (hollow trees) or stone shelters (rocks or buildings) situated close to lakes, rivers and ponds where it hunts. Summer and winter roosts may be far apart. Sometimes the animal will spend the winter on the ground under a stone. In mountains it is present up to altitudes of 1500 m.

Food and reproduction The large feet allow Daubenton's bat to catch both small invertebrates and fish at the surface of water. It will also consume emerging aquatic insects. At the time of reproduction the females can form colonies of 100 individuals.

TRACES AND OBSERVATION

Observation This species is one of the most common in western Europe. It can be found near water, under old bridges or in ancient mills. It is, however, secretive. Its flight is rapid and manoeuvrable, and close to the surface. This bat is capable of swimming and taking off again from the surface of the water, while a pipistrelle which falls into water has to swim to the bank before it is able to fly again.

1 The pond bat
2 Capaccini's bat

RELATED SPECIES

Brandt's Bat
Myotis brandti

Previously confused with the whiskered bat, this species was not identified until 1971. Its precise distribution is unknown and information on its biology is still lacking.

The long–fingered bat (Capaccini's bat)
Myotis capaccinii

Strictly Mediterranean, it has a limited distribution in Europe. It is found from Spain to Italy as well as in Yugoslavia and on the Mediterranean islands, and is a social species mixing with other bats such as *Miniopterus*. Little is known of its biology but it seems to prefer to live near water. Similar to Daubenton's bat, it has large feet.

The pond bat
Myotis dasycneme

A species of northern and eastern Europe. In winter it migrates as far

1 Brandt's bat.
2 The lesser mouse–eared bat.

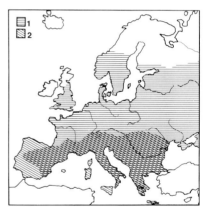

south as the northeastern border of France. Linked to damp areas, it hunts above the water over ponds and lakes. It is also found hunting over fields and along the edges of forests. Although larger, it resembles Daubenton's bat.

The lesser mouse–eared bat
Myotis blythi

Despite its name this small *Myotis* is difficult to distinguish from the larger species. Present in the south of France and in Corsica, it forms colonies with the greater horseshoe bat.

THE WHISKERED BAT
Myotis mystacinus

FAMILY VESPERTILIONIDAE

ECOLOGY AND BIOLOGY

Distribution Widely distributed in Europe the whiskered bat is only absent from the north of Scandinavia and the south of Spain.

Description Total length 6.5–8.5 cm of which 3–4 cm are tail; forearm 30–37 mm; wingspan 20–22 cm; weight 4.5–8 g.

A small bat, which could be confused with a pipistrelle. The pelage is more grey and it has tufts of hairs at the corners of its mouth which are a characteristic feature.

> **Similar species** *The common pipistrelle.*

Habitat and territory This species prefers edge areas —the borders of woods, forests and rivers, and also living close to man. In summer it uses roof spaces and attics, like the common pipistrelle.

Food and reproduction The whiskered bat catches small butterflies and flies. At the time of reproduction, in summer, the females gather in small colonies in hollow trees, under a roof or between rocks. Their reproductive cycle is similar to other European species of bats.

TRACES AND OBSERVATION

Observation This bat is small and not easy to observe. Nearly always cavernicolous, it can be found suspended by its feet or squeezed into crevices. In flight, because of its small size, it can be confused with the common pipistrelle. It emerges during the early evening and has a rapid take off. Its flight is light and silent. Hunting occurs close to the ground or at a height greater than that of the common pipistrelle. It is often found near trees, where it lands from time to time to capture prey, or over water.

> **Risks of confusion** *With other small* Myotis *and pipistrelles which can be seen at the same time.*

1 The whiskered bat.
2 Geoffroy's bat.

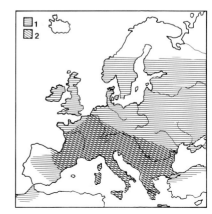

GEOFFROY'S BAT
Myotis emarginatus

FAMILY VESPERTILIONIDAE

ECOLOGY AND BIOLOGY

Distribution An inhabitant of mid–western Europe. This species is absent from Great Britain and from a large part of central and northern Europe. Present almost throughout France but is not found in Brittany.

Description Total length 8.5–9.5 cm of which 4–4.5 cm are tail; forearm 36–42 mm, wingspan 22–24 cm; weight 7–15 g.

The external border of the ears of this species is deeply notched, hence its Latin name.

> **Similar species** *All other small* Myotis *bats.*

Habitat and territory Found in relatively open habitats, parks, gardens, and grasslands but also close to trees.

Food and reproduction This species feeds mainly on spiders and small insects. The reproductive colonies can reach several hundred females. The species seems more social than other Myotines.

TRACES AND OBSERVATION

Observation A gregarious species, often found in granaries and habitually suspended by their feet from the roof of their roost. The emarginated bat is a little less discreet than some related species. It also emerges early in the evening. Its flight is low and agile, flying at about five metres above ground. This species does not seem to move far between summer and winter roosts. The latter roost must be warmer (between 4.5–9°C).

Often associated with the greater horseshoe bat in summer, this species has also diminished considerably.

NATTERER'S BAT
Myotis nattereri

FAMILY VESPERTILIONIDAE

ECOLOGY AND BIOLOGY

Distribution Widespread throughout most of Europe.

Description Total length 7.5–9.5 cm of which 3–4.5 cm are tail; forearm 35–43 mm; wingspan 22–27 cm; weight 6–14 g.

The ears of Natterer's bat, a species difficult to identify are intermediate in size and shape between those of Bechstein's bat and the Geoffroy's bat.

> **Similar species** *Other* Myotis *spp.*

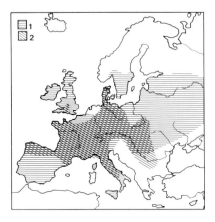

1 Natterer's bat.
2 Bechstein's bat.

Habitat and territory This species is found in lightly wooded, hilly countryside, in parks, gardens and in urban habitats. It often roosts in hollow trees in summer and in underground shelters in winter (crevices in walls, drill holes in mines).

Food and reproduction Natterer's bat eats mostly flies and weevils captured from the surfaces of leaves. The groups of females in reproductive roosts consist of only a few dozen individuals.

TRACES AND OBSERVATION

Observation This bat is usually very secretive. It begins to hunt relatively late in the evening making regular passes around the tops of trees or over water. Its wing beats are relatively slow. Although it is one of the most widely distributed of European bats the amount of information on its biology is scant.

BECHSTEIN'S BAT
Myotis bechsteini

FAMILY VESPERTILIONIDAE

ECOLOGY AND BIOLOGY

Distribution This species is found in Corsica, southern Britain and most of central Europe, but is absent from the more northern and southern regions of the continent.

Description Total length 7.5–10 cm of which 3.5–4.5 cm are tail; forearm 39–47 mm; wingspan 25–28 cm; weight 8–12 g.

This species has the largest ears of any *Myotis* and may easily be confused with the long–eared bats.

> **Similar species** *The long–eared bat.*

Habitat and territory Found in woods and forests, this bat may also use subterranean shelters in winter.

Food and reproduction This species hunts forest insects, in flight or on the foliage of trees. The females form small reproductive colonies.

Observation Bechstein's bat is rare in much of its range and leaves few traces of its presence. It hides in crevices and hibernates alone. It can be observed in the early evening when it flies slow and low through the forest. It can also be seen when prospecting the foliage or spaces between trees.

THE SEROTINE
Eptesicus serotinus

FAMILY VESPERTILIONIDAE

ECOLOGY AND BIOLOGY

Distribution Found practically throughout Europe. Although its range does not extend as far north as Scandinavia, it was recorded for the first time in 1982, in the extreme south of Sweden. In Great Britain it is only found in southern England.

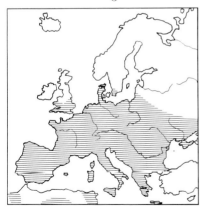

The common serotine.

Description Total length 10.5–14 cm of which 4.5–6 cm are tail; forearm 48–57 mm; wingspan 34–36 cm; weight 17–35 g.

The serotine is a large bat resembling a giant pipistrelle. The dorsal pelage is dark brown but the belly is lighter; the face and the wing membrane are black. The ears are not well developed, the tragus is short, rounded and narrow. The extremity of the tail extends slightly beyond the membrane.

Similar species *Northern bat and the common noctule.*

1 *The northern bat.*
2 *The parti–coloured bat.*

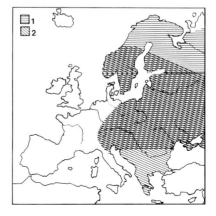

Habitat and territory This species is frequently found in open countryside, parks and gardens of rural areas. It seeks roosts in the holes in trees, as well as in buildings, but only in the colder parts of its range will it occupy caves and underground shelters. This species can reach altitudes of up to 1500 m in mountainous regions. At present, in western Europe it appears to be closely linked to human habitation, even seeking roosting sites in towns. It is almost exclusively anthropophile in the Low Countries. It is possible that this species is in the process of extending its range northwards to, for example, Great Britain and Scandinavia.

Food The serotine eats mainly large insects, captured in flight often close to foliage. Butterflies, moths and beetles form the basic diet.

Reproduction The reproductive cycle of the serotine is comparable to that of other species (mating in autumn, fertilisation in early spring, single births in May or June). The reproductive colonies, usually found in buildings, include only females (about 20–30 adults). Males pass the summer separately.

TRACES AND OBSERVATION

Indications of presence The serotine is more difficult to find when roosting in trees than when it is roosting in buildings. It is quite a secretive species using narrow holes to exit and enter. A brown mark around a hole is an indication of the presence of this bat. Under a roof the serotine habitually hangs from the highest beams and it is possible to hear the noise of movement on the timber. It regularly colonises new buildings (e.g. roosting in the expansion joints or air ducts) and can pass both summer and winter in the same place. The droppings measure 6–8 mm long by 3 mm wide.

> **Risks of confusion** *With colonies of noctules.*

Observation Emerging at nightfall, the common serotine remains secretive even during movement. It circles trees (in gardens, parks, open woodlands) at a distance of 30–40 m diameter with slow wingbeats.

RELATED SPECIES

The parti–coloured bat
Vespertilio murinus

Little is known about this species which has a limited distribution to the east of the Juras and Isere. This bat is brightly coloured and noisy, especially at the time of mating in autumn. In summer the males are more gregarious than the females.

The northern bat
Eptesicus nilssoni

A nordic species, it is a little smaller than the common serotine. In the southern part of its distribution it is found at altitude and in the north its range extends up to the polar circle of Scandinavia.

THE COMMON NOCTULE
Nyctalus noctula

FAMILY VESPERTILIONIDAE

ECOLOGY AND BIOLOGY

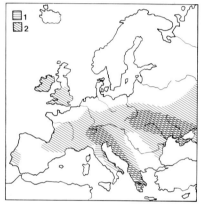

1 *The greater noctule.*
2 *Leisler's bat.*

Distribution Widely distributed in Europe, this bat is only absent from Ireland, Scotland, the north of Scandinavia and the north west quarter of

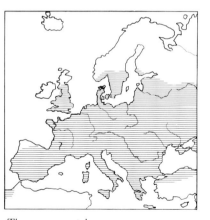

The common noctule

Spain. The exact distribution is difficult to ascertain.

Description Total length 11–14 cm of which 4–6 cm are tail; forearm 45–48 mm; wingspan 33–40 cm; weight 15–40 g.

Large and robust, this bat appears more stocky than the common serotine which is about the same weight. Its head is massive, ears clearly separated and the small rounded tragus is mushroom–shaped. The pelage is red–brown and more vividly coloured than other species in the region and is a little lighter below than above. The long narrow wings give the bat a characteristic silouette.

> ***Similar species*** *The common serotine, large noctule and Leisler's noctule.*

Habitat and territory The common noctule is often found in trees and forests, and also lives near towns. It can also be found in grasslands where there are hollow trees. In mountains it is found up to altitudes of 1300 m but does not occur above the level of broadleaved and mixed forests. It occurs more rarely in coniferous forest.

Food It has a mixed diet consisting of butterflies, beetles, grasshoppers and crickets, captured in flight.

Reproduction Typical common noctule colonies consist of 20–100 females accompanied by their young, roosting in hollow trees. Up to a thousand animals have been counted living together in some buildings. The males remain isolated at this time. The reproductive cycle is similar to that of other bats in the region.

TRACES AND OBSERVATION

Indications of presence In a forest, a colony of common noctules will cir-

culate between several roosts. The entrance, often a woodpecker hole, is soiled by bat droppings. A noisy species, the individuals of a colony may emit incessant cries during the day. When there are several hundred bats this is easily heard.

> **Risks of confusion** *With some colonies of serotines which occupy similar roosts.*

Observation The common noctule is the first bat to emerge in the evening and so is relatively easy to observe, especially with binoculars. The silhouette is characteristic. When hunting the flight normally describes large circles in the sky about 100 m in diameter, between 10 and 40 m above ground. Although its flight is not rapid it can make a succession of spectacular dives in pursuit of prey. These dives allow it to pick up speed, at the end of

The common pipistrelle. The most common of our bats often seen flying round lamp standards in the evening.

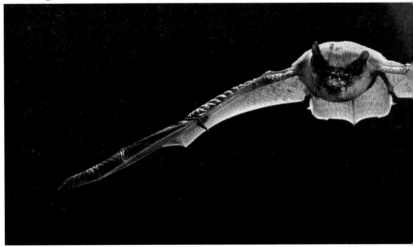

which it regains height and begins hunting again. It can also hunt close to the ground. Noctule bats fly in small groups and the hunting areas can often be a long way from the roosts. The hibernation roosts are sometimes situated at a long distance from the site of reproduction – up to several hundred kilometres. The species is migratory.

RELATED SPECIES

Leisler's noctule
Nyctalus leisleri

Leisler's noctule, although small, is very similar to the common noctule. It has a pointed head and the colours of the back and belly are more contrasting although less bright. Its biology is poorly known despite its wide distribution. Preferring forests, it adopts hunting strategies similar to those of the common noctule.

The greater noctule
Nyctalus lasiopterus

This is the largest species of European bat. Its wingspan approaches 50 cm and forearm length nearly 7 cm. Its distribution and biology are almost unknown. Some unconfirmed observations have suggested that they occur in the south of France. One specimen was discovered in Brittany in 1987 and another in the Dordogne the same year. It is a forest species.

THE COMMON PIPISTRELLE
Pipistrellus pipistrellus

FAMILY VESPERTILIONIDAE

ECOLOGY AND BIOLOGY

Distribution It is found throughout Europe – except in northern Scandinavia – and on the Mediterranean islands and in northern Africa.

Description Total length 5.5–9 m of which 2.5–3 cm are tail; forearm 27–34 mm; wingspan 18–23 cm; weight 3–8 g.

The smallest and probably the most abundant bat in Europe. General shape is rather round, ears and tragus moderately developed, pelage brown–red above becoming grey below, and the wing membranes, ears and muzzle are black.

> **Similar species** *Other pipistrelles and small vesper bats.*

Habitat and territory The common pipistrelle can be found in most habitats. In the Alps it can be found up to altitudes of 2000 m. This species can live near houses and penetrate towns, even the hearts of large cities (e.g. Paris).

All the sheltered places in houses can be used for roosts – spaces between stones, under tiles, in false roofs, under shingles, and behind shutters. They also use tree trunks but

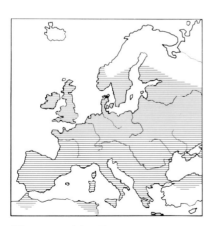

The common pipistrelle.

are rarely seen in caves in western Europe.

In summer the females form large reproductive colonies separate from

the males which are less gregarious. Several successive roosts can be occupied in a summer season. The hibernation roosts are quite different and may be tens or hundreds of kilometres from the summer roosts.

Food The pipistrelle is insectivorous and hunts on the wing, feeding on small moths and dipterans in particular.

Reproduction As with many other bats in the region mating takes place at the end of summer. It seems that for a time the animals become somewhat territorial. Other matings may take place during the winter. Fertilisation is delayed until spring. The gestation period is about 55 days but may be extended if weather conditions and food supply are unfavourable. One or possibly two young are born in June. The relatively low reproduction rate is compensated for by the longevity which has been recorded up to 16.5 years although the average is around 2–3 years.

TRACES AND OBSERVATION

Indications of presence:

ROOST: European pipistrelles do not construct nests but occupy regular roosts depending on season. A colony of about 50 bats living in a wall, in gaps behind wooden shuttering, will leave a trace of brown clearly visible on a floor used day after day. Approaching the hole in daytime a tiny metallic squeak can be heard. There is an increase in activity in the colony just before a flight. Their particular odour also helps to detect colonies.

DROPPINGS: the accumulation of guano below the summer roosts of this species can be used to find these roosts. The droppings measure 5 mm long, are cylindrical, rounded at both ends and include the remains of insect skeletons. They quickly become dry and friable.

> **Risks of confusion** *With indications left by other pipistrelles and the majority of small bats that live near man.*

Observation The common pipistrelle is easy to see when it lives near man. To find a colony during the summer it is only necessary to position oneself at sunset and wait for the animals to emerge one by one. They have a fast zig–zag flight. This species hunts regularly by the light of street lamps, over gardens and between buildings.

Savi's pipistrelle
Pipistrellus savii

Slightly larger than the common pipistrelle and a little more southerly in distribution than Kuhl's pipistrelle. Its

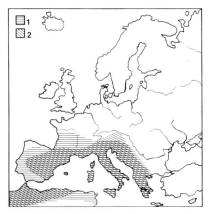

1 Kuhl's pipistrelle
2 Savi's pipistrelle

distribution in France is limited to the Mediterranean area. The animal is seldom seen and its biology is poorly known.

RELATED SPECIES

Kuhl's pipistrelle
Pipistrellus kuhli

A little larger and slightly lighter in colour than the common pipistrelle, this species lives in southern Europe from Spain to Greece. The light edging of the wing of pipistrelles between the fifth finger and the foot is particularly clear in this species.

NATHUSIUS'S PIPISTRELLE
Pipistrellus nathusii

FAMILY VESPERTILIONIDAE

ECOLOGY AND BIOLOGY

Distribution Nathusius's pipistrelle lives throughout continental Europe and as far north as southern Sweden. It is localised in Spain and Portugal. This species is rarer in western than in eastern and central Europe, and is not common in France. It is also found in Corsica.

Description Total length 8–9.5 cm of which 3.5–4 cm are tail; forearm 32–37 mm; wingspan 23–24 cm; weight 6–15 g.

A little bigger than the common pipistrelle, Nathusius' pipistrelle is difficult to distinguish from the other species. Precise identification depends on examination of the teeth.

Similar species *The other pipistrelles.*

Habitat and territory The pipistrelle most preferring forests and trees in summer. It makes long journeys, probably true migrations, which bring it south for winter. The record for an individual ringed in USSR and found in France three months later was 1600 km from its origin.

Food and reproduction This species feeds on insects caught during flight.

Its reproduction is similar to that of the common pipistrelle.

OBSERVATION

Observation It is necessary to search for this animal in holes in trees, although the roosts are seldom found. Its preference for forests sometimes leads it to shelter between the drying planks at sawmills. This type of refuge is a convenient one for those individuals from eastern Europe arriving to pass the winter in France.

Risks of confusion *See the common pipistrelle.*

Nathusius's pipistrelle.

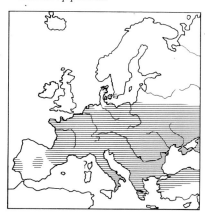

THE BARBASTELLE
Barbastella barbastellus

FAMILY VESPERTILIONIDAE

ECOLOGY AND BIOLOGY

Distribution Widely distributed in Europe, extending north to Great Britain and Scandinavia. It is absent from Greece, as well as from parts of Spain and Italy. Although it is not found in northern France it is present in Corsica.

Description Total length 8.5–11.5 cm of which 4–5.5 cm are tail; forearm 36–43 mm; wingspan 24–29 cm; weight 6–14 g.

The large ears of the barbastelle join above the eyes and give the head a

Habitat and territory This species seeks colder habitats – up to 2000 m in the Alps – but is found at lower altitude in the northern parts of its range. Always found near water.

Food and reproduction Its food preferences are little known. It has a small mouth and probably eats small dipters in flight. Equally, little is known about its reproduction. Mating takes place in autumn and winter; the breeding colonies consist of 10–20 females, each giving birth to two young.

OBSERVATION

Observation Often solitary, roosting in holes in trees or at the mouths of caves, the barbastelle leaves few traces. Its resistance to cold allows it, in winter, to find refuge at the entrances to underground holes. It is necessary to search for this species in the small entrance holes of tunnels and caves. It may live close to man. In flight the animal appears heavy, flying nearly straight, always about 3 m above ground. It hunts regularly over water.

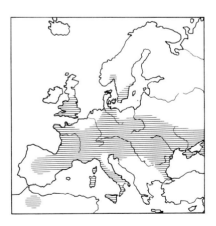

The barbastelle.

characteristic appearance. The pelage is brown–black and a little lighter on the belly.

THE COMMON LONG–EARED BAT
Plecotus auritus

FAMILY VESPERTILIONIDAE

ECOLOGY AND BIOLOGY

Distribution It has a more northerly distribution than the grey long–eared bat and is found over a wide area of Europe. It lives in most areas of Scandinavia, Great Britain and Ireland, is common in France but is absent from Spain, Greece, southern Italy and the Mediterranean islands.

Description Total length 8–10 cm of which 3.5–5 cm are tail; forearm 35–42 mm; wingspan 22–28 cm; weight 5–11 g.

The enormous ears of this species are characteristic. Only the long pointed tragus can be seen when, at rest, the animal folds its ears.

> ***Similar species*** *The grey long–eared bat and Bechstein's bat.*

The common long–eared bat.

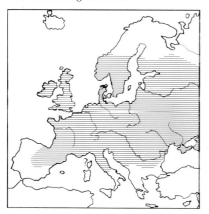

Habitat and territory The common long–eared bat is more tree-loving than its close relative, the grey long–eared bat, roosting in trees. It is found up to altitudes of 2000 m in the Alps and Pyrenees.

Food and reproduction This species feeds on insects captured in flight or gathered from foliage. Its reproductive cycle is comparable to that of other species of bats.

TRACES AND OBSERVATION

> ***Risks of confusion*** *With the grey long–eared bat and the lesser horseshoe bat, which behave rather similarly.*

Observation Not very gregarious, this bat is difficult to find. The reproductive colonies may have only a few dozen females, and the males stay nearby. Individuals hibernate alone.

Rare in Southern Europe. The common long–eared bat flies in a characteristic manner. It is capable of hovering, exploring a tree, leaf by leaf, or patrolling close to a wall to seek out resting insects. Its ears, pointing forwards, are characteristic of the animal. In free flight its shape is similar to that of the lesser horseshoe bat. It can land on the ground or on a branch to gather insects. It emerges to hunt late in the evening.

THE GREY LONG–EARED BAT
Plecotus austriacus

FAMILY VESPERTILIONIDAE

ECOLOGY AND BIOLOGY

Distribution Absent from the north of Europe, this species inhabits the extreme south of England, Spain, France, Portugal, Greece.

Description Total length 8.5–11 cm of which 4.5–5.5 cm are tail; forearm 37–44 mm; wingspan 25–29 cm; weight 6–10 g.

The grey long–eared bat is very similar to the common long–eared bat except that it is a little larger, its feet are relatively smaller and the pelage is a little greyer. The ears and tragus are not the same colour in contrast to the common long–eared bat.

> **Similar species** *The common long–eared bat and Bechstein's bat.*

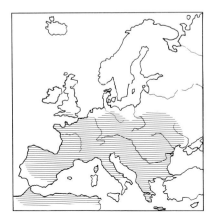

Habitat and territory The grey long–eared bat is found mostly in cultivated areas but is found more frequently in buildings than the common long–eared bat. It seems to prefer old houses and churches. In the Alps it is absent above 1400 m.

Food and reproduction See the common long–eared bat.

OBSERVATION

Observation Solitary in winter, more gregarious in summer, this species leaves little trace of its presence. It lives in warmer and more open places than the common long–eared bat and is more often seen than the latter in the south of France. Its hunting flight is very similar to that of the related species. It systematically explores the foliage of trees. Often it consumes large prey which it takes to a particular spot to which it often returns to rest. The debris which accumulates under these feeding areas may be the best indication of its presence.

> **Risks of confusion** *See the common long–eared bat.*

The grey long-eared bat.

The common long-eared bat. (page 108) ▶

SCHREIBER'S BAT
Miniopterus schreibersi

This is one of the most widely distributed bats in the world. Inhabiting southern parts of Europe it can be found in the south of France, from the Rhone valley to the Atlantic. Also present on Corsica. Medium sized (wingspan about 30 cm), it can be recognised by its rounded head and long narrow wings. Its flight resembles that of swallows. It hunts in groups over open ground. A strong flier, it can move over long distances to find a hibernation roost. A hibernation roost of 50 000–70 000 individuals has been discovered in Aude.

Schreiber's bat.

CARNIVORES

THE WEASEL
Mustela nivalis

FAMILY MUSTELIDAE

ECOLOGY AND BIOLOGY

Description Total length of male 23–30 cm of which 5–6.5 cm are tail, female 20–25 cm of which 4–5.5 cm are tail; weight of male 60–170 g, female 35–90 g.

The weasel is the smallest of the European carnivores. Sexual dimorphism is marked, as can be seen from the measurements. These measurements should be reduced for the dwarf form. The pelage is brown above and white below with a sinuous line of

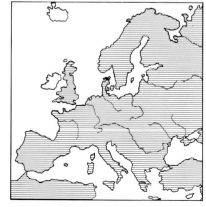

The weasel.

demarcation on the flanks. It can be confused with the stoat in summer pelage. To separate the two species it is neccessary to look at the tail. In the weasel it is short and plain coloured, whereas in the stoat it is long and black tipped.

Distribution The weasel is present throughout Europe with the exception of Iceland and Ireland, at sea level through to altitudes of 2700 m. Two forms of the species are recognised – a dwarf form in northern Europe and the normal form in southern Europe.

> **Similar species** The stoat.

Habitat and territory Its habitat is very varied and it is found everywhere there are small rodents, but is less abundant in the great forests and on high mountains. It frequents many hedgerows and walls, but suffers less than the stoat from changes in agriculture. Its small size allows it to inhabit a variety of vacated rodent holes.

The territory of the weasel ranges from 1–100 ha depending on the density of prey, with males having a larger territory than females.

Food The weasel eats mostly small rodents, in particular the field vole. These represent 58–99% of the diet. Birds, amphibians and insectivores make up most of the remainder. Capable of passing through a hole 15 mm in diameter, the weasel chases rodents through their own underground burrows, under piles of wood or under snow.

Reproduction First matings take place in spring and litters of 2–10 young are born after a gestation period of 35 days. If prey is abundant it can produce another litter during the summer. Young born in spring attain sexual maturity at the age of four months and they too can produce young in late summer. The capacity for reproduction in weasels is high, not a common feature amongst carnivores.

TRACES AND OBSERVATION

Indications of presence

PRINTS: each foot of the weasel has five clawed digits. The prints measure about 1 cm broad and 1.5–2 cm long. It is very difficult to find the footprints except in snow, so it is preferable to study the trail to confirm the identity of the animal. The size of the prints, grouped together at each leap are very variable and close to those of the stoat. To confirm it is a weasel it is best to measure the length of the bound, on average less than 30 cm. When moving in snow the weasel jumps from side to side. The marks which it leaves in the snow are oblique whilst those of the stoat are straight.

DROPPINGS: with a diameter of 2–3 mm the droppings are more or less cylindrical, twisted and tapering at the end. Length 3–8 cm. Taking into account the pronounced dimorphism in these small mustelids and the regular increase in the size of different species it is difficult to distinguish the faeces of a male weasel from those of a female stoat. The size of the two individuals is close and their faeces are of the same dimensions.

> **Risks of confusion** With the faeces and prints of the stoat.

Observation Active all year round the weasel is often diurnal. It can be seen along roads, hedges and walls, and at the edge of fields and grasslands. There is no particular season which is best for observing this species. It is neccessary to look in areas where many rodents are known to occur, especially voles: Weasels and stoats will probably be seen entering rodent burrows and coming out with a rodent in the mouth, which they carry to their nest.

The weasel can be caught in traps, though it is neccessary to check whether permission for this is required. It is essential to open the traps frequently to release the animal before it wounds itself or dies from stress.

The weasel slides easily into the burrows of rodents.

THE STOAT
Mustela erminea

ECOLOGY AND BIOLOGY

Distribution This is an animal with a northern distribution. The stoat is present in Canada, northern USA, Greenland and in the greater part of northern Asia. In Europe its distribution extends south to the north of

Spain, Portugal and Italy. In France it is absent from the Mediterranean fringe and Corsica.

Description Total length of male 28–43 cm of which 6–12 cm are tail; of the female 26–35 cm of which 6–8 cm are tail; weight of male 130–450 g, of female 130–280 g.

In summer the pelage of the stoat is brown above and yellowish on the belly with a distinct demarcation line. The tail has a black tip all the year round. In winter the pelage of stoats living in cold regions becomes white; for those living on the plains and in areas with milder winters the hair colour remains brown throughout the year, though it lightens a little in the winter. The change of colour takes place at the spring and autumn moults. During the change, irregular patches of colour give an unusual appearance to the pelage.

> **Similar species** *The weasel, the polecat and the mink.*

Habitat and territory The stoat inhabits all areas that provide numerous holes and where small rodents are plentiful. For this reason it is less common in grasslands and agricultural areas with cereal crops but takes advantage of the favourable conditions in farmlands, open forests and marshes.

The stoat nests under thick bushes,

low walls, stones, hedges or in quiet farm buildings close to villages. It can travel up to 8 km to find its food. The territory of the females is on average less than 10 ha, whilst the range of males covers 10–35 ha depending on the density of prey.

Food The stoat can be considered a specialist predator of rodents. It preys primarily on voles on the European continent, and on the rabbit in Great Britain and Ireland. It also captures birds, insects, worms, etc. The stoat gathers stocks of food near its nest allowing it to survive through the winter.

Reproduction Mating occurs from May through to July, but the stoat does not give birth for another 7–12 months because of delayed implantation of the embryo. The gestation period is 20–28 days. The stoat has only one litter per year with 4–18 young (average 8). The populations show large fluctuations directly linked to the density of available prey.

Comparison between the pelage of the stoat and that of the weasel:
1 the stoat in summer;
2 the stoat in winter;
3 the weasel all year round.

TRACES AND OBSERVATION

Indications of presence

PRINTS: it is rare to find good stoat tracks except in the snow. The five digits on each foot are only occasionally visible on the prints. The forefoot measures measures 2 x 1.5 cm and the hindfoot 3.5 x 1.5 cm. As the stoat

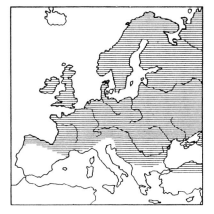

The stoat.

bounds through snow the marks go two by two – the hindfeet are placed in the prints of the forefeet. The trail resembles a sinuous line of double prints. The distance between each group of prints is usually over 30 cm but varies between 20 and 80 cm.

DROPPINGS: similar to those of the weasel but larger. They are composed of bones, hair and feathers; twisted and tapered at one end, measuring 5–8 cm long and 5 cm wide. They are found on walls and stones all along the paths taken by the stoat, particularly where these cross.

> **Risk of confusion** *the faeces and prints left by the weasel and the polecat are similar to those left by the stoat.*

Observation The stoat is active all year round, but in winter it is more nocturnal and in summer diurnal. They are easily captured in traps placed along walls and hedges (see weasel). They can sometimes be seen in broad daylight chasing rodents or moving along trails at the edges of fields. They are found regularly in areas where vole plagues occur, during periods of high density (see field vole) and one sees them entering the galleries of voles and soon returning carrying a vole by the neck. At harvest time they hunt the small rodents around mills. When one finds a breeding nest it is sufficient to stay at a little distance, well camouflaged, to see them several times a day bringing prey to the young.

The western polecat. (page 116) ▶

THE WESTERN POLECAT
Mustela putorius

FAMILY MUSTELIDAE

ECOLOGY AND BIOLOGY

Distribution The western polecat is present throughout Europe except in northern Scandinavia, Iceland and Ireland. It is no longer found in Greece nor on the Mediterranean islands. The distribution is very even throughout Europe except in Great Britain where it has been scarce for some decades.

Description Total length of male 48–62 cm of which 10–16 cm are tail; of the female 42–50 cm of which 10–13 cm are tail; weight of male 750–1600 g, of the female 430–840 g.

The polecat is distinguished at first glance from other mustelids by the colour of its fur; it is the only member of the family in which the underparts of the body are darker than the upper parts, notably the belly, the legs and the tail which are black while the colour of the back is brown and that of the flanks more or less yellow. The head of the polecat has three obvious white patches, from the front and in profile there is one on the muzzle, another under the eyes and a third on the end of the ears.

> **Similar species** *The steppe polecat, the marbled polecat and the American and European minks.*

Habitat and territory The polecat frequents all sorts of habitats but shows a marked preference for wet areas and the banks of rivers. It is common near human habitation especially

in areas of severe climate and where there are brown rats. The destruction of the hedgerows and woodland on old agricultural properties is the principal cause of scarcity. The two types of

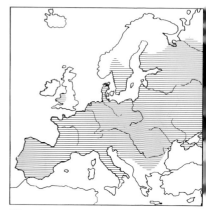

The polecat.

habitat least frequented by the polecat are the cereal plains, which lack shelter, and the great forests. In a place where prey is plentiful the polecat may remain for long periods but it regularly makes long nocturnal journeys of several kilometres.

Food Although mainly carnivorous, the polecat has a varied diet. The bulk of its food consists of voles, mice, rats and rabbits. After the otter and the mink it is the carnivore which eats the greatest number of cold–blooded vertebrates (e.g. fish and frogs).

Reproduction Breeding takes place in March–April. The young, 2–12 in number are born in May–June after a gestation period of about 42 days. At the time of birth, the female prepares the nest in the shelter of a hollow tree, a pile of hay, a heap of stones or an abandoned rabbit burrow, lining it with hairs, feathers and dry herbs.

> ***Risks of confusion*** *With the prints of the mink, the otter and medium sized mustelids.*

TRACES AND OBSERVATION

Indications of presence

PRINTS: the size of the polecat prints are very similar to those of the mink, and between those of the stoat and the marten. In mud, the footprint measures 3.5 cm long by 2.5–4 cm wide depending on the spacing of the digits. The size may double in snow where the trail is easier to recognise. When bounding, the polecat groups the four feet, and most of the time each imprint is separate from the others, while in the martens the hindfeet often land in the tracks of the forefeet. The trace of the tail can often be seen at the level of the foremost feet.

DROPPINGS: twisted and drawn out, they measure 6–8 cm long and about 1 cm wide and contain hairs, bones, feathers and sometimes scales and some fish bones. The droppings can be easily confused with those of the otter but the odour of the polecat droppings is sickening while the otter droppings smell sweet.

SLAUGHTER: the polecat makes reserves of food which it leaves in particular places. The most striking example is the 'slaughter' of frogs. From time to time, on the banks of rivers or near the den of a polecat, dozens of frogs or toads can be found, either killed or simply paralysed following a bite to the spinal chord. The otter also attacks frogs and toads but it eats the whole frog and only leaves the head and skin of toads. In the slaughters of the polecat almost complete frogs or partially eaten frogs are found.

Observation Active all year round, the polecat can be seen like the weasel and the stoat in regions of high prey density. The period of greatest activity is at dusk when they can be found near rabbit warrens or on the banks of a river.

After a flood, traces of polecat are frequently seen on the banks, where they have been searching for fish and small animals killed by the current. In spring, the time of the breeding season, the animal is less timid and moves about to find places where frogs are breeding, returning for several days.

RELATED SPECIES

The steppe polecat
Mustela eversmanni

The steppe polecat, also called the Siberian polecat, lives in the semi–arid and steppe zones of Russia and central Asia. Its distribution extends to the plains of eastern Europe, where it overlaps with the distribution of the European polecat in Rumania, Bulgaria, eastern Austria and Yugoslavia. The steppe polecat has a similar colouration to the European polecat – darker below than above – but the pelage is much lighter and the head almost white. Measurements and traces are the same for both species, and for the marbled polecat

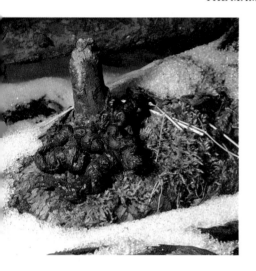

The marbled polecat
Vormela peregusna

The marbled polecat is found in the same areas as the steppe polecat. It is present in eastern Europe, Bulgaria and northeastern Greece. It is distinguished from the others by its patchy pelage of brown and cream on the flanks. The underparts are darker, as in the other species.

A polecat toilet.

THE FERRET
Mustela furo

FAMILY MUSTELIDAE

ECOLOGY AND BIOLOGY

Origin and description The ferret is a domestic albino form of polecat; both are about the same size. The precise origin of the ferret is unknown, and experts differ on whether it is the descendent of the European polecat or the steppe polecat. A study of the chromosomes has shown that it is more closely linked to the former than to latter. The ferret can be crossed with the polecat and the descendants are fertile. The progeny of these crossings have very variable colours – from the creamy white of the domestic type to the nuances of dark brown, comparable to those of the wild polecat, passing through all the intermediates.

OBSERVATION

Observation The ferret is a domestic animal directly dependent on man and used for hunting rabbits in their holes. However, some individuals having escaped or been set free deliberately, have formed small populations. This happens only occasionally in Europe, except on some of the islands of Britain, in Sicily and Sardinia. Ferrets that have returned to the wild state take on an appearance close to that of the polecat and the traces which they leave are exactly the same.

The best example of introduction is New Zealand where the ferret was released in an attempt to limit the populations of rabbits. In that region it remains an abundant wild species.

> ***Risks of confusion*** *See polecats.*

THE EUROPEAN MINK
Mustela lutreola

FAMILY MUSTELIDAE

ECOLOGY AND BIOLOGY

Distribution The distribution of the European Mink is rapidly diminishing. It is divided today into two zones: a small area in the west of France and the extreme northwest of Spain, and a large area in Russia and eastern Europe from Finland to Rumania.

Description Total length 46–60 cm of which 13–19 cm are tail; weight of male 650–1000 g, of female 475–800 g.
   The pelage of the European mink is uniformly brown except for a white mark on the chin and the upper lip. The male is a little larger than the female. It is difficult to distinguish from the American mink but the American mink does not have white on the upper lip only on the chin. It is usually neccessary to have the animal in the hand to identify it with a certainty. The European mink has one to several patches of white on the neck and the chest especially animals from the east of the range.

> **Similar species** *The polecat and the American mink.*

Habitat and territory The European mink inhabits wet areas – estuaries, marshes, canals, lakes, ponds and water courses and it has a preference for bodies of water and rivers in wooded areas. The animal nests in crevices in the banks but it also occupies the abandoned tunnels of aquatic mammals such as the muskrat. Little is known about its territorial behaviour. In Russia individuals have a territory of 20–100 ha, including 2.5 km of river.

Food The mink eats all sorts of prey living in wet habitats – rodents, amphibians, fish, birds, crustaceans. In winter when snow and ice make it difficult to find food, several individuals may concentrate on river banks, where the water is flowing.

Reproduction The period of sexual activity begins early in the year, starting at the end of January and lasting until April. The gestation period is 35–72 days, on average 50 days. In April to May litters of 2–7 young are born. The female may give birth to a second litter if the first is lost.

TRACES AND OBSERVATION

Indications of presence
PRINTS: resemble those of the polecat and have about the same dimensions (3–4cm long, 3–4.5cm wide) and the track is similar. The principal difference is that the European mink has five digits on each foot linked by one

pad which indicates its aquatic lifestyle. The complete footprint, showing all five digits, the claws and the pad is only visible in soft mud where every detail remains fixed.

DROPPINGS: measuring 6–8 cm long by 5–8 cm wide they are difficult to distinguish from those of the polecat especially when the mink has eaten an animal with feathers or hair. When the polecat eats fish or frogs the droppings are more formless whilst those of the mink are more cylindrical.

> ***Risks of confusion*** *With droppings of the polecat, the American mink, martens, and otter spraints.*

Observation The European mink has become extremely rare in western Europe so there is little chance of seeing it in the wild (and then it is difficult to distinguish from the American mink). Most sightings are of animals killed on the roads.

THE AMERICAN MINK
Mustela vison

The mink and the polecat can be distinguished by the white markings on the head: 1 the European mink; 2 the American mink; 3 the polecat.

FAMILY MUSTELIDAE

ECOLOGY AND BIOLOGY

Distribution and habitat The natural distribution of the American mink is the greater part of North America. After its importation to Europe to supply the fur trade, at the start of the twentieth century,

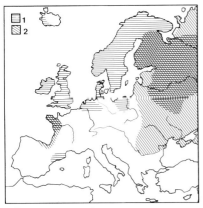

1 The American mink.
2 The European mink.

numerous animals escaped and many farms were abandoned allowing the mink to establish populations in many European countries. It is now a 'wild' species common to Iceland, Scandinavia, France, Great Britain and USSR. This range is expanding and it will soon be found in other European countries. It lives equally near inland waters, or at the edge of the sea where it nests amongst rocks.

The introduction of the American mink is causing concern to zoologists, who believe that the animal will occupy the ecological niche of the European species at the expense of the latter, as has happened in USSR.

Description The American mink closely resembles the European species except that it is a little larger and does not have the white mark on the upper lip.

TRACES AND OBSERVATION

Observation The tracks and the faeces of the American and European mink are similar and they cannot be distinguished by traces. In Britain the mink makes dung heaps on rocks at the edge of the sea near its den. One can confuse the faeces of the mink with those of the polecat and with the spraints of the otter after eating fish.

> ***Risks of confusion*** *See the European mink.*

THE BEECH MARTEN
Martes foina

FAMILY MUSTELIDAE

ECOLOGY AND BIOLOGY

Distribution The beech marten is found throughout continental Europe except Scandinavia. In the north it is absent from Ireland, Iceland and Great Britain and in the south from Corsica, Sardinia, and Sicily. It is present on Crete, Cyprus, Corfu, Rhodes, and the Balearic Islands.

The beech marten, a capable climber.

Description Total length 66–77 cm of which 23–27 cm are tail; weight of male 1.7–2.5 kg, of female 1.1–1.5 kg.

The pelage of the beech marten is lighter than that of the pine marten and varies from brown to greyish beige.

Similar species *The pine marten, the mink and the polecat.*

Habitat and territory In the northern part of its distribution the beech marten is closely linked to human activity. It lives in or close to villages. It often makes its nest in heaps of straw or in a quiet corner of an agricultural building. It is regularly discovered in towns and suburbs. When not close to human habitation the beech marten lives in hollow trees, woodpiles, heaps of stones or rabbit holes. In the south of its range the beech marten may live far from human habitation in rocky areas which are probably its natural habitat. In these habitats the range may extend over several hundred hectares, whilst near human areas the range only covers about 100 ha on average, giving a radius of activity of about 600 m around the den.

Food The beech marten is almost omnivorous, feeding on small mammals, birds, eggs, fruit, insects and all sorts of rubbish left by humans. The emphasis of its diet changes from meat in winter to fruit in autumn.

Reproduction Mating takes place in summer. The egg is fertilised immediately but does not implant in the uterus for a further 8 months, in February or March. At the end of a gestation period of about 56 days, 2–7 young are born (average 3).

The toilet of a beech marten is sometimes found in a barn full of hay.

TRACES AND OBSERVATION

Indications of presence

PRINTS: similar in all respects to the pine marten but the digital pads are naked and the print appears clearer (see pine marten).

DROPPINGS: very similar to those of the pine marten (4–10 cm long by 1 cm broad) although the droppings of the beech marten more often contain cherry stones and remains of human food. Some claim that the droppings have a stronger odour than those of the pine marten but this remains unproven.

LATRINES: the position of latrines is a good indicator of its presence. The beech marten may leave its droppings at random, like the pine marten but, for preference, it defecates regularly at the same place, for example near the nest in the hay stack in which it lives or on the floor of a granary.

NEST: when the beech marten finds shelter in straw its nest is placed in the lower parts of the stacks which are never used. The entrances and exits of the holes are about 12 cm in diameter. If the stack is too small to build tunnels the beech marten arranges a simple nest in the form of a bowl. Close to the nest there are droppings and remains of food, corpses, broken eggs and other debris.

Risks of confusion *With prints and droppings of the pine marten and the polecat in its natural habitat.*

Observation When the nest is found there is a good chance of seeing the animal. It is neccessary to take up a position before nightfall as close as possible to the exit the beech marten uses to leave to go hunting. When the young begin adventuring from the nest in June or July they are noisy and less shy, like the adults in the mating season. It is possible to attract a beech marten by regularly offering food always placed in the same spot.

1 The beech marten.
2 The pine marten.

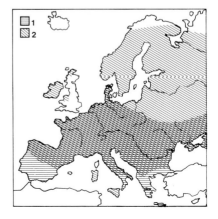

THE PINE MARTEN
Martes martes

FAMILY MUSTELIDAE

ECOLOGY AND BIOLOGY

Distribution The pine marten is found throughout Europe with the exception of the southern Iberian peninsula, Greece and Iceland. It is rare in Great Britain and is restricted to certain regions of Scotland and Wales.

Description Total length 62–82 cm of which 22–27 cm are tail; weight of male 1.2–2.5 kg, of female 0.8–1.4 kg. Confusion between the pine and beech martens is common. It is therefore easier to describe the two species simultaneously. The beech marten, larger than the pine marten, has shorter legs, smaller and rounder ears. The pelage of the pine marten is sleeker and darker than that of the beech marten because of the long brown hairs which give a better covering to the grey fur.

The most commonly used criteria for identification are the white patches on the throat but this character is not constant and many intermediate forms exist.

The martens both have on the throat and chest a bib of a lighter colour which contrasts clearly with the rest of the darker fur. In the pine marten this area is mostly of an orange colour, has an irregular contour and forms an area of colour which stops at the level of the shoulder or descends slightly between the forelegs (see diagram). The bib of the beech marten is white and shows a clearer line of demarcation than that of the pine marten, and extends lower, separating into two lobes which cover the upper part of the front legs. The soles of the feet of the pine marten are adapted to its arboreal way of life. The digital pads and the plantar arch are long and covered with long hairs, especially in winter. In the beech marten the pads are naked and finer to allow better adhesion to rocks, walls or pipes which it regularly climbs.

On examining the skull it is possible to identify the species by the teeth of the upper jaw. In the pine marten the external border of the third premolar is concave whilst in the beech marten it curves outwards. The only reliable aid, one which can only be obtained from a dead male, concerns the length of the baculum *(os penis)*. In the pine marten it measures less than 46 mm, while in the beech marten it reaches 61 mm.

Habitat and territory The pine marten is typically a forest dweller. It lives in both coniferous and broad leaved forests, in low and high country. It is estimated that for the animal to thrive a minimum area of 30 ha of forest, sufficiently far from human disturbance, is necessary.

The population density is about one individual per 100 ha. The area of vital range varies, depending on the richness of the area and available prey, from 200 ha in lowland forest in France to 800 ha in the north of Scandinavia.

The nests are usually found high in trees, in holes or in the old nests of birds or squirrels.

A

A Comparison of the bibs of:
1 The pine marten; 2 The beech marten.

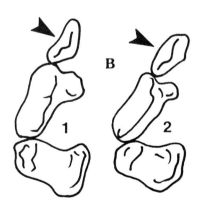

B

B Comparison of the dentition of the same species.

Reproduction The marten has delayed implantation, retarding gestation for 8 months. The female thus only gives birth once a year to a litter of 2–7 young (average 3) in March to May, the mating having taken place in the previous summer. In danger, the female leads the young to another nest and guards the entrance.

Food Small rodents make up more than 75% of the marten's food, supplemented, especially in winter, by birds. At the end of summer and autumn fruit and insects are included in the diet.

TRACES AND OBSERVATION

Indications of presence

PRINTS: there are five digits on each foot but the prints commonly show only four. These measure 4–5cm long by 3–4 cm wide. In snow the hairy feet leave prints twice as large. It is convenient therefore to see the trail to identify the animal.

TRAIL: The marten's trail has a variable shape which sometimes resembles that of a hare or fox. If one follows the trail for some metres it may stop at the base of a tree that the animal has climbed, this minimises the risk of confusion with other more terrestrial species. When it bounds in the snow the marten always places the hindfeet in the tracks of the forefeet thus the track is composed of a series of double imprints disposed obliquely each 60–80 cm apart.

DROPPINGS: measure 10 cm long by 1 cm broad, and contain much hair and feather. They are very twisted and are often folded and tapered at one end. They are found every 100–200 m along forest paths either on the soil or on some eminence or stone. Sometimes the marten will leave droppings in the fork of a tree or on rocks overlooking the country, like genets, but the droppings of genets are much larger.

Observation The marten is difficult to see. It lives in a habitat where the foliage is usually closed and is normally active at night. It may be possible to

The droppings of the marten are twisted.

find a nest where young are present in May, June or July but one must be careful as the marten is very shy and often changes its nest.

One can also, armed with a pair of binoculars and much patience, post oneself at a path through the forest.

***Risks of confusion** With the prints of the beech marten, polecat, fox and hare in the snow and the droppings of other mustelids and the genet.*

◀ *The pine marten.*

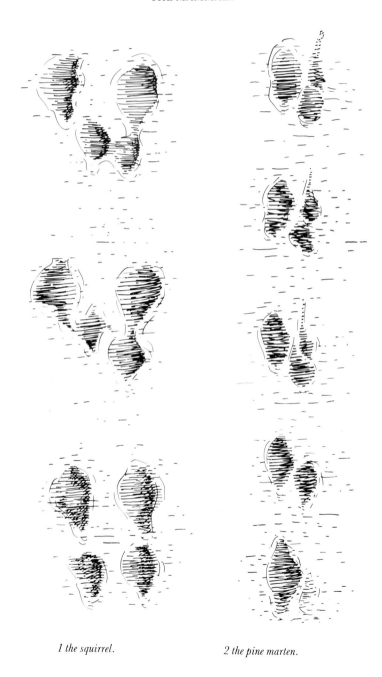

1 the squirrel.   *2 the pine marten.*

Tracks in the snow.

THE OTTER
Lutra lutra

FAMILY MUSTELIDAE

ECOLOGY AND BIOLOGY

Distribution Only one species of otter is found in the rivers and on the coasts of Europe. It is found throughout Europe, in north Africa, in the USSR and in the greater part of Asia and Indonesia. In Europe the population is considerably reduced and it is only satisfactorily maintained in four countries: Ireland, Scotland, Portugal and Albania. Throughout its range it occurs in scattered populations.

Description Total length 0.9–1.20 m of which 30–40 cm are tail; weight of male 6–12 kg, of female 4–8 kg.

The species is well adapted to an aquatic life. The fur, which is exceptionally dense, is brown on the back and lighter underneath the belly and the throat. The long and supple body, short legs terminating in webbed feet, flat head and long strong tail allow it prowess in water.

Similar species *Muskrat and coypu.*

Habitat and territory The otter lives in any suitable water habitat, from the sea to lakes at altitudes up to 2500 m. Today it is also found in the wetlands which do not dry out and in streams near their source.

The otter marks its territory with urine and faeces (which are called spraints). The territory can cover 10 km of river for females and 50 km for males. That of the male can encompass several female territories but all may be visited by wandering individuals (young or non–reproductive), which makes it impossible to recognise individuals from spraints and difficult from prints.

The otter.

Food From studies of the diet of European otters three important features have been found:

1) the preponderance of prey is fish(50–90%)
2) the otter adapts to locally abundant food
3) seasonal abundance of prey is important

As soon as frogs come together in numbers to reproduce they become the principal prey of otters. Crayfish

An otter swimming.

are much appreciated where they occur and mammals (water rats, muskrats), birds and reptiles are only complementary prey. In attacking, by priority, the most abundant prey, the otter plays a balancing role in the general equilibrium of animals.

Reproduction Otters only attain sexual maturity at 2–3 years of age and females have only one litter each year but the birth may take place at any time of year. The number of young is usually 1–3, rarely more. The young stay with the mother for seven months

The print of the otter, showing the five well–spaced digits.

The otter holt is often found under tree roots at the edge of the water.

to one year, and she brings them up alone.

TRACES AND OBSERVATION

Indications of presence The traces which the otter leaves in its habitat are, in order of importance: spraints, footprints, shelters, runs, and remains of meals. All are found close to water.
SPRAINTS: small glutinous masses, green or black, bristling with fish scales and bones of fish and frogs. When dry they become white and fall apart. In the fresh state their odour, sweet for carnivore faeces, evokes that of linseed oil mixed with fish. They cannot be confused with any other species except the faeces of a polecat or a mink which has eaten fish. However otter spraints are less regular in shape,

whilst those of the polecat and mink are twisted and of definite size as well as having a nauseous smell.

The spraints are left side by side on stones at the edge or in the middle, of the water on sand banks, tufts of vegetation, or on all the obstacles that occur on its travels.
PRINTS: each foot has five digits arranged in a fan–shape around the plantar arch. These are almost round and all make marks at different levels so that a line from the outer digital pads passes below the middle three pads. If compared to the print of a badger, which also has five digits, the same line would cut the central pad at its base (see drawing). The claws rarely make any marks.

The musk rat and the coypu also have 5 digits but their prints are lengthened by the long claws which give the print a star–shaped aspect. The size of the forefoot of an adult otter can be drawn within a circle 6 cm in diameter, whilst the hindfoot leaves a heelprint, measuring 6–7.5 cm. All these measurements can be increased by 2 cm for a large adult male. The tracks left by the young less than seven months old, measure less than 5 cm across.

TRAILS: these run along the banks of rivers and lakes and across bends in streams and rivers. To distinguish them from the runs of large rodents (e.g. coypu or muskrat) it is neccessary to find the spraints scattered along the path.

Risks of confusion With prints left by mink, muskrat, coypu and badger.

Observation Of all wild carnivores the otter is the most difficult to see except in Norway, Ireland and Scotland, where it is often seen by day, especially on sea coasts. If one can find the holt the best time of day to watch is at the start of activity at dusk in winter and in the hour before dusk in summer. The most favourable times for observing otters are: the night and day following the draining of a pond when otters will come to eat any fish trapped in the mud, when frogs come to the ponds to breed and in winter, near frozen ponds which it crosses on its travels.

THE BADGER
Meles meles

FAMILY MUSTELIDAE

ECOLOGY AND BIOLOGY

Distribution The badger is found throughout Europe with the exception of northern Scandinavia, Iceland and the Mediterranean islands (Sicily, Sardinia, Corsica etc).

Description Total length 75–95 cm of which 15–20 cm are tail; height at shoulder 30 cm; weight of male 9–20 kg, of female 6.5–14 kg.

It is impossible to confuse the badger with any other mammal as its shape and colour are characteristic. Its massive body, short strong legs and small tail give it a clumsy bearing, making it look more like a bear than a mustelid. Its grey fur is made up of long straight hairs. Two black bands are visible on its white head beginning slightly below the muzzle encircling the eyes and ears then becoming broader on the neck. The white tips of the ears accentuate the black and white contrast of the head.

Habitat and territory The badger lives in deciduous woodland, mixed forests and wooded areas in open country or on mountains up to 2000 m. The preferred habitat is where forests and open plains meet. The position of the set is determined by the security of the place, the abundance of food and the proximity to water. The badger lives in groups of 5–12 members. Each group occupies a territory of 50–400 ha; in favourable areas the density can reach 5 individuals per square kilometre.

Food The badger is omnivorous, adapting its feeding to local and seasonal resources. It eats both animal and vegetable food including small mammals, frogs, insects, molluscs, tubers, fruit, mushrooms and cereals. Recent studies have shown that it will also eat large quantities of earthworms – up to 200 in a single night.

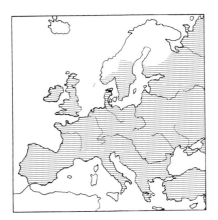

The badger.

Reproduction As in some other mammals reproduction in the badger involves delayed implantation of the blastocyst. Mating takes place during February and March and gestation is retarded by 10 months, the young are born at the beginning of the following year, during winter. There are 2–7 young in a litter (average 3).

TRACES AND OBSERVATION

Indications of presence Except in winter, when the badger remains inactive though not hibernating, it leaves the most obvious traces.

PRINTS: there are five digits on each foot, armed with strong claws. The print of the forefoot measures 4.5 cm broad by 5 cm long. The claws of the forefeet, which are used for burrowing, are very long and make an impression 1 cm in front of the pads. The hindfeet have shorter claws, but the nail always leaves a print, making the length of the trace 7.5 cm instead of 4.5 cm.

The track is wider than that of the fox. The feet, slightly turned inwards, are not placed in the same line. The badger patrols its territory and follows habitual paths. Repeated passage over the same route leaves obvious paths radiating from the set and leading to latrines.

DROPPINGS: the badger regularly defecates in the same place – called the latrine. One can see dozens of small holes about 20 cm diameter and 5–10 cm deep in which the badger deposits a dropping 4–8 cm long of irregular form, sometimes cylindrical like that of a fox and sometimes soft and formless. They are not covered.

SET: a badger set that has been used for many generations may consist of hundreds of metres of tunnels with as many as 30–40 entrances. Dozens of tonnes of earth thrown out modify the

The den of a badger has a trench in front.

appearance of the whole area. The main entrance consists of a large trench 30 cm deep which continues for several metres to the outside. Often grasses and leaves (old bedding) can be seen outside the entrance which the badger has dragged out to clean its set. **SCRATCHINGS:** all along its diggings the badger makes numerous scrapes, looking for acorns, insects, etc. It

The badger leaves its droppings in a hole dug for the purpose.

destroys anthills and wasps nests in order to eat the eggs and developing young.

HAIRS: are often left stuck to barbed wire. They are long, straight, black and white, and easy to find.

> **Risks of confusion** *With the prints left by the otter and the domestic dog, and the faeces of the fox, the racoon dog, domestic dog and wild cat.*

Observation Observation of the badger away from its set is very difficult. The best place to see it is in the immediate area of the diggings. The badger leaves the set regularly at dusk during spring and autumn, and an hour earlier in summer. When the young begin to explore their neighbourhood in May or June one can watch them play and groom in front of the entrances to the set. It is not always necessary to have a hide to see badgers, remaining perfectly still is often enough if the observer stays downwind.

A good method of remaining undetected is to climb a nearby tree some two hours before dusk and wait patiently without moving.

The genet (see page 139).

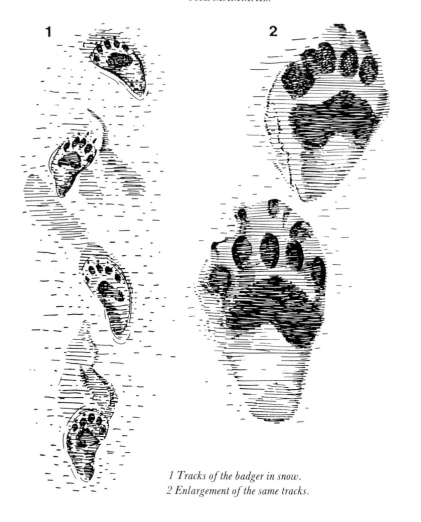

1 Tracks of the badger in snow.
2 Enlargement of the same tracks.

THE GLUTTON
Gulo gulo

FAMILY MUSTELIDAE

ECOLOGY AND BIOLOGY

Distribution The glutton inhabits the northern regions of Alaska, Canada and Russia. In Europe it is only found in northern Scandinavia where its population is diminishing.

Description The total length of body 0.80–1.20 m of which 12–30 cm are tail; height at shoulder 45 cm; weight 15–35 kg.

The glutton is the largest of the mustelids. Its massive shape reminds one of a small bear or a large badger. The females are smaller than the males.

The brown colour of its fur contrasts with a white patch on the front of the jaw and with the yellowish band that runs along its flanks from the elbow to the base of the tail. There is little risk of confusion with other species.

Habitat and territory The glutton inhabits the wildest areas from the swamps of the taiga to the high wooded mountains. The male occupies an enormous territory of about 500–2000 km^2 in which it will not tolerate the presence of other adult males. Its range can include those of several females. Its den is found amongst rocks or under trees.

Food The food of the glutton is very varied and includes small vertebrates, such as voles or frogs, and large animals such as red deer, reindeer or elk. In winter it manages to survive by attacking wounded or feeble ungulates and eating carrion. The female gives birth to one litter of two or three young each year.

TRACES AND OBSERVATION

Indications of presence

PRINTS: these are in proportion to the size of the animal. Each foot of the glutton has five digits armed with strong claws. The prints measure 8–15 cm long by 7–12 cm wide depending on whether they are found in mud or snow. Only rarely does the claw of the forefoot make a mark. The track in snow is easy to recognise. When the glutton moves in bounds, it groups its feet in fours leaving behind a series of long deep holes spaced 60–90 cm apart. When five digits are visible in the print it resembles that of the otter but when one digit is missing it resembles that of a wolf.

DROPPINGS: twisted and full of hairs they measure 15 cm long by 2 cm wide. They are dropped in an irregular fashion.

> **Risks of confusion** With the prints and faeces of the otter, the badger and the wolf.

Observation The glutton is both nocturnal and diurnal, but as it has such a vast territory it is difficult to find, even in winter.

THE GENET
Genetta genetta

FAMILY VIVERRIDAE

ECOLOGY AND BIOLOGY

Distribution An African animal that reached Europe at the time of the Saracen invasions, accompanying the men who conquered the region. In Europe it is found in Portugal, Spain and the southwestern corner of

France. Some isolated individuals and some small populations have been reported to the west and north in Germany, Belgium and in the Alps.

Description Total length 0.80–1.06 m of which 40–48 cm are tail; weight 1.3–2kg.

The pelage of the genet is remarkable; on a foundation of clear grey, a black stripe runs all along the dorsal spine and four or five rows of black longitudinal stripes decorate the flanks. The breast and the belly are grey; the tail is ringed with 10–12 black rings. The male is a little larger than the female.

Although larger, it is possible to confuse the genet with the wild cat. The genet, however, has a longer tail, almost as long as the head and body, and the ears are larger (4.5 cm). In addition its fine muzzle is circled by a characteristic black line.

The droppings of a genet can reach 25 cm in length ▶

The den of a genet amongst rocks.

THE MAMMALS

> **Similar species** *Wild cat.*

Habitat and territory The genet shows a preference for quiet areas with dense vegetation far from human habitation or rocky areas with many holes. It can also be found in undisturbed areas of pine forests and marshes. It is absent from areas of harsh climate or persistent snow.

The genet builds a nest in piles of rocks, caves, hollow trees or ruins. During the day it rests in the tops of bushy–topped trees, like some of the conifers or leafy trees such as the chestnut.

Food The genet is a strict carnivore. In the Balearics it eats lizards, which are abundant, but small mammals are normally the main diet, especially the field mouse (although very agile and a woodland species) while other carnivores catch more field voles. The genet is a remarkable climber, and will also feed on dormice, squirrels and birds.

Reproduction For the genet the breeding season begins mainly at the beginning of the year but the females can give birth twice a year at almost any time. Only two or three young are born which begin to leave the nest at about 8 weeks old. On these early excursions many genets are killed on the roads or are easily taken in the traps set for martens.

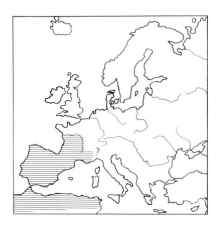

The genet.

Tracks made by the genet in mud.

TRACES AND OBSERVATION

Indications of presence

PRINTS: footprints of genets are rarely found as they live mostly in trees and on rocks. Because of their distribution the chances of finding prints in snow are very limited. Each paw has five digits and the claws are semi-retractable. The forefoot of the genet measures 3 x 2.5 cm, the hindfoot 3 x 3 cm. The four upper digits are disposed evenly above the plantar pad the fifth digit, small and eccentric, only rarely leaves a mark. The track resembles that of a domestic cat. When it climbs the genet leaves claw marks on tree trunks. These claw marks may be confused with those of the squirrel, the marten and the wild cat.

DROPPINGS. these are the most useful traces, the most frequent and the most easy to find. The faeces are very large for an animal of this size, they measure from 10–24 cm long and 1.5–2 cm in diameter. They are always laid in a horseshoe shape and end in a tuft of blades of grass. Black when fresh, they whiten and decay with age. Their odour is not as unpleasant as those of the cat. The 'toilets' or middens are also characteristic. The genet habitually defecates in the same place – on a shelf of rock or in the forks of branches overlooking their range. The middens can also be found on artificial promontories in flat places (sheds,

hunting platforms, etc). The toilets are used by several genets and can contain dozens of faeces of various dimensions depending on the age range of the animals.

> **Risks of confusion** *With the faeces of domestic cat, marten, fox and dog, and the prints of the cat.*

Observation The genet is nocturnal and difficult to see, as it changes lair from time to time except during the gestation period. They are most frequently seen when on the move at night in the headlights of cars.

THE EGYPTIAN MONGOOSE
Herpestes ichneumon

FAMILY VIVERRIDAE

ECOLOGY AND BIOLOGY

Distribution and habitat Of African origin, the mongoose now occupies southern Portugal and Spain where it lives in the scrub, rocky zones and bushy hills. It was introduced to the island of Miget on the coast of Yugoslavia.

The Egyptian mongoose.

Description Total length 0.80–1 m of which 35–50 cm are tail; weight 3–7 kg. The mongoose is recognised by its slender shape, pointed muzzle, grey–brown fur and its very long tail which ends in a point.

Food The diet of the mongoose is varied, based on small vertebrates – rodents, birds, frogs. It also successfully kills poisonous snakes, because it is very quick and resistant to the effects of the poison.

TRACES AND OBSERVATION

Observation The feet of the mongoose are very small for an animal of this size. The prints measure about 3 x 3 cm. The finger pads are naked and end in long curved claws. Of all the European carnivores the mongoose is the most active during the day. It sleeps amongst rocks or bushes or in abandoned burrows.

THE WILD CAT
Felis silvestris

Family Felidae

ECOLOGY AND BIOLOGY

Distribution The wild cat is widely, but fragmentally distributed throughout Europe. Five separate zones can be distinguished. The two largest are in the southern part of the continent – to west in the Iberian peninsula and to the east in Greece, Yugoslavia, Bulgaria, Hungary and Rumania. Several distinct areas make up a third zone in Italy and the Mediterranean islands. Further north the wild cat is found in the northeast of France (Champagne, Ardennes, Burgundy, Lorraine) and to a lesser extent in Germany and Poland. Lastly a small population remains in Scotland, the most northerly part of the European distribution.

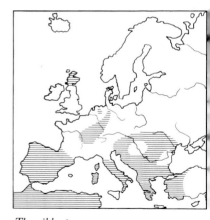

The wild cat.

Description Total length of male 78–100 cm of which 26 cm are tail, of the female 73–90 cm of which 25–32 are tail; weight of male 3.5–7.7 kg, of the female 2.5–5.2 kg.

The wild cat is larger than the domestic cat and the difference seems greater because of its thick coat. The

The wild cat.

basic colour of the pelage is a grey–brown, more or less dark, with a scattering of black spots and lines. Two fine lines of black appear on the cheeks, the higher of the two cutting the eye. Five black lines begin on the forehead and descend to the neck, passing between the eyes. The bands, which cover the upper flanks, are not always well defined, in contrast to the stripe which runs along the back from the neck to the base of the tail. The tail is tufted and thick throughout its length, is ringed with black and ends in a thick black tip. Only the last two rings, closest to the tip, are well marked.

It is quite difficult to distinguish the wild cat from a large striped domestic cat. Usually the black stripe on the back of the the domestic cat continues onto the base of the tail, which ends in a point. The only reliable criteria are a combination of complex measurements of the cranium.

> **Similar species** *the domestic cat, the genet and the lynx.*

Habitat and territory In the scientific literature the name forest cat is tending to replace that of wild cat. This change is due to the fact that the habitat of the cat is now better known – the animal shows a preference for broad-leaved and mixed forests. In woodland the cat inhabits the dense undergrowth near clearings, meadows and grasslands. It is also found in the dry forests of plateaux that have wet gorges, but areas of permanent snow limits the range of the species towards the north by preventing hunting. Males occupy a territory of 200–1200 ha within which one can find several female ranges of 130–300 ha.

The den of the wild cat is arranged in thick bushes, hollow trees, rocks or abandoned buildings.

Food The principal prey of the wild cat are small rodents which it captures by hiding and stalking like domestic cats. Although it is an excellent climber it rarely hunts in trees. In Scotland where the snow lasts through the winter and would normally constitute a handicap, the cat eats mainly rabbits which it pursues into their burrows under the snow.

Reproduction Mating takes place in mid–January to mid–February. Births are in April after a gestation period of 63–69 days. On average three kittens are found in a litter. In winter, and to give birth, the wild cats use the holes of foxes and badgers, which explains the accidental gassing to which they are sometimes exposed.

TRACES AND OBSERVATION

Indications of presence

PRINTS: although the forefeet of the wild cat have a fifth digit, it is placed very high and the prints only show four toes separated evenly around the plantar pad. The general form of the print is circular, a little longer than broad (4.5 x 3.5 cm) These dimensions are slightly larger than those of a domestic cat (3 x 3 cm) but it is practically impossible to distinguish one from another.

SCRAPES: the retractile claws of the wild cat do not mark the ground but leave traces on the trunks of trees where the animal climbs. The wild cat tends to scratch at the same place. Careful observation may reveal the old scars at the foot of a scratching post.
DROPPINGS: those of the wildcat measure up to 20 cm long by 1.5–2 cm wide. They have the peculiarity of being composed of several distinct parts linked to each other. The cat may also leave droppings in view on a prominence or covered in a trench.

> **Risks of confusion** With the prints left by the domestic cat, the genet and the lynx, and with the faeces of the fox, genet, badger and domestic cat.

Observation The wild cat is a suspicious animal and very discreet. It hunts an hour before dark. The tracks in the snow are one of the only useful methods for finding its lair. The best time to see the animal is when it is in a tree, which happens either if chased by dogs and is seeking refuge or when taking a sun bathe stretched along a branch. In either case it can be seen for a while before hiding again.

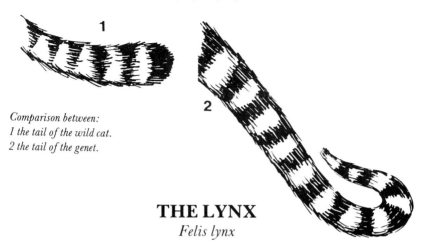

Comparison between:
1 the tail of the wild cat.
2 the tail of the genet.

THE LYNX
Felis lynx

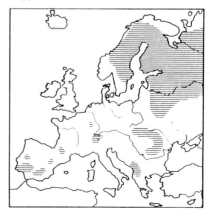

Family FELIDAE

ECOLOGY AND BIOLOGY

Distribution In Europe the distribution of the lynx is very fragmented. Small populations are found in the south of Spain, the Pyrenees, Yugoslavia, Greece, Czechoslovakia and Rumania. Larger populations are found in Scandinavia and Russia. The lynx has been reintroduced to Switzerland, West Germany (Bavaria) and in the Voges in France; the Swiss population now colonises the Jura mountains in France.

Description Total length 0.90–1.55 m, of which 10–25 cm are tail; weight 15–40kg.

The pelage of the lynx is reddish or greyish, more or less spotted with black markings. The male is a little larger than the female. The lynx is larger than the wild or domestic cat, has a short tail ending in a black tuft and has a tuft of black hairs at the tip of the ears.

The Iberian form or Spanish lynx *(Felis lynx pardina)* which is sometimes considered to be a separate species shows more contrast between the black markings and the ground colour.

> **Similar species** Domestic and wild cats.

Habitat and territory Usually found in lowland or mountain forest, but in the south of its range it can also be found in rocky and dry habitats.

The lynx

147

Food and reproduction The prey of the lynx is very varied, ranging from small rodents to deer, through to birds and small carnivores, up to the size of the badger.

Mating occurs in spring and the young (usually 2 or 3) are born at the beginning of summer.

TRACES AND OBSERVATION

Indications of presence
PRINTS: similar to those of cats but larger (6–8 cm wide and long). The digital pads are evenly distributed around the front of the plantar pad. The claws do not make marks.

DROPPINGS: in shape similar to those of the fox but wider (2–3 cm) and longer (up to 25 cm). The lynx leaves droppings in specific places like the badger.

> **Risks of confusion** *With the traces left by the dog, wild and domestic cats, and the racoon dog. The droppings are similar to those of the fox and the feral dog.*

Observation Solitary and nocturnal, the lynx is particularly difficult to watch. Even scientists with radio tracking equipment seldom see these animals.

THE FOX
Vulpes vulpes

FAMILY CANIDAE

ECOLOGY AND BIOLOGY

Distribution Of all the European carnivores, the fox is the most widespread. It is found everywhere except Iceland and Crete.

Description Total length 0.90–1.23 m of which 33–43 cm are tail; weight of male 7 kg (up to 11 kg), of the female 6 kg.

The fox is smaller than usually thought because of its thick fur, particularly in winter. The colour, usually red, can vary individually from yellowish to dark brown. The black

varieties, belong to the same species as the red fox.

> **Similar species** *The arctic fox, the wolf and the racoon dog.*

Habitat and territory The fox lives in a wide range of habitats from forest to plains. It is also found more and more in the cities and suburbs (Paris, London, Oslo, Madrid). It uses dens for giving birth and to hide from danger but most of the time the fox lies up in thickets, rocks, woodpiles, etc.

The lynx.

The first sortie of one of a litter of foxes.

The fox is very adaptable, and occupies a territory which can be very diverse in form and extent – from 50 ha in suburban districts to 1300 ha in grassland areas. The vital range extends from 300–400 ha. The average density is about one per 100 ha, however, with the presence of rabies in Lorraine, France, for example, the density has fallen to one per 600–1000 ha.

Food The favourite prey of the fox are rabbits and voles, but with an important element of fruit, earthworms and domestic rubbish, which can be especially important in winter.

The fox.

During the rearing period the fox can bring to the lair prey of considerable size. One can find remains of meals all round the lair, contrary to the badger which does not leave any remains near its den.

Reproduction Mating takes place in January and the gestation period is 53 days. Litter size can be 3–7 young, but more usually 4–5. The family group consists of the adult pair, but in areas of abundant prey the male may have 5–6 females, of which only one, the dominant female, assures reproduction, while the others help to raise the young.

TRACES AND OBSERVATION

Indications of presence
PRINTS: fox prints are common in the mud along roads as well as at the edges of rivers in summer and in snow in winter. The prints show four digits in a regular pattern although the fox has five digits on the forefeet and four on

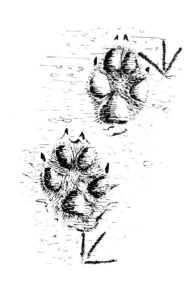

Footprints made by the fox in mud.

The straight trail of the fox in snow.

on the same line. When the animal bounds its groups the feet by four, the track resembling that of a hare. When trotting the feet are grouped by two, one hindfoot and one forefoot placed side by side (see marten).

DROPPINGS: disposed all along the territory, most often on small hummocks (stones , tufts of grass, heaps of earth) well in sight. They measure 10 cm long and about 2 cm wide. Shape and colour are variable depending on diet but generally fox droppings are less twisted and less slender than those of mustelids.

LAIR: differs from the badger set by having an opening plunging directly into the soil without an access trench.

Risks of confusion *With the prints of the dog and the faeces of mustelids, wild cat, racoon dog and genet.*

---

the hindfeet. In winter the underside of the feet are covered with long hairs and are more spread making the prints larger and less sharp. The prints measure 5 cm long by 4–4.5 cm wide and are easily confused with the prints of a small dog. To distinguish between them it is necessary to look at the position of the digital pads: in the fox the two centre digits leave marks in front of the two exterior digits, so that a line traced between the upper parts of the two lateral pads passes cleanly above the base of the two central pads. The same line on the print of a dog cuts the two central pads in the midline or the lower part. The small claws often leave a trace 2 mm in front of the print. **TRACK:** is narrow and sinuous. The fox places its feet 25 cm apart almost

Observation Although much fox activity takes place at night it is one of the animals which can be encountered by chance on walks or seen from hides. The two best times of year to see them are spring and winter. In April–May it is possible to see the young in front of the lair and the parents hunt frequently to find prey for them.

In winter the fox cannot hunt voles, and it is then that it often approaches human habitation and will travel long distances.

A good observation post, although lacking romance, is near public rubbish tips, which foxes frequent throughout the year. During the mating season foxes can be heard howling.

RELATED SPECIES

The arctic fox
Alopex lagopus

Limited in Europe to the mountains of Scandinavia and to Iceland, the arctic fox looks like a small fox with short ears. The pelage of the animal is white in winter and brown in summer. Some individuals, much sought after by furriers, have a dark grey coat in summer and blue grey in winter. In Iceland the arctic fox is common but in Scandinavia it is becoming rare while at the same time the red fox is extending its range northwards.

THE WOLF
Canis lupus

FAMILY CANIDAE

ECOLOGY AND BIOLOGY

Distribution During the last few centuries the distribution of the wolf has been considerably reduced. Almost everywhere it is in retreat. There remain several isolated populations in Spain, Portugal, Italy and in the south of Scandinavia. From Russia eastwards the distribution is more continuous.

Description Total length 1.40–1.80 m of which 30–40 cm are tail; height at shoulder 0.60–0.80 m; weight 20–50 kg.

The wolf resembles a large dog. Its forequarters are large and its broad head is surmounted by small ears. In repose its long tail falls along the rump and is not curled as in the domestic dog. The colour of the pelage varies from almost black to white, but is usually grey.

> **Similar species** *The jackal and the domestic dog.*

Habitat and territory From the steppes of southeast Europe to the tundra of the north, the wolf exhibits a facility for adaptation. It roams a vast territory, the size of which depends on the amount of food available.

Food and reproduction The wolf has very varied prey and hunts small rodents as well as elk. It also eats invertebrates, fish and does not disdain carrion. In southern Europe – Spain and Italy – it can find food in domestic rubbish.

An adult pair is the basic social group, and the whole group participates in rearing the young, averaging 3–6 per litter, born after a gestation period of 62 days.

TRACES AND OBSERVATION

Indications of presence
NEST: often found in natural cavities, but the wolf can dig its own lair or enlarge already existing holes which it uses only for giving birth and caring for the young.
PRINTS: are similar to those of a large domestic dog but the digits are more

The wolf.

widely spaced and the powerful claws make clear marks. There are four digits on the fore– and hindfeet. The trail is straight. The footprint measures about 12 cm in diameter.

DROPPINGS: measuring 10–15 cm long and 2–3 cm in diameter, the droppings of the wolf contain masses of hair and bits of bone. They may be left in the open or hidden and covered with earth like a dog.

The wolf.

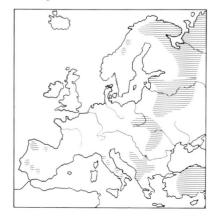

Risks of confusion *Tracks and droppings of the wolf resemble those of a domestic dog and a jackal.*

Observation The wolf is one of the most difficult European mammals to see and requires a great deal of patience. It is necessary to find a place where the animal is known to occur. A good indication can be obtained by examining the hackles of local sheep dogs; if they are raised in sharp points it is reasonable to suppose that wolves frequent the area. It is possible to discover recently killed prey, to stay nearby and wait silently, taking note of the wind direction, for the wolf to return.

RELATED SPECIES

The common jackal
Canis aureus

The common jackal is not found exclusively in the warmer regions but can be found in the Balkan peninsula, and from the Black Sea to the Adriatic. There is also a population in Hungary. Similar to a medium sized dog (weight about 12 kg on average, shoulder height 40–50 cm) the jackal has brown fur sometimes tinged with red. It can be found near towns but is very retiring. An inhabitant of open environments (steppes, areas of cultivation) it is also found in wet areas (marshes, reedbeds).

1 The arctic fox.
2 The common jackal.

THE RACOON DOG
Nyctereutes procyonoides

FAMILY CANIDAE

ECOLOGY AND BIOLOGY

Distribution The natural range of the racoon dog is the Far East (eastern China, Korea and Japan). Between 1923 and 1950, some 9000 specimens were released in the USSR. Since then they have colonised parts of Europe and their area of distribution has increased by 1.5 million km^2. Today they are abundant in Poland, Finland and Rumania and they continue to expand to the west. They are often found in the Federal Republic of Germany, Austria and France where the first individual was seen, in the Department of Aisne in 1979.

Description Total length 50–80 cm of which 15–20 cm are tail; height at shoulder 20–25 cm; weight 7 kg.

The general appearance of the racoon dog resembles a fox in size and a badger in its massive body. It can also be confused with the racoon because both species have a black facial mask around the eyes. But the racoon has a longer tail ornamented with several black rings. The racoon dog has whiskers which hang from its cheeks and the ears, paws and tail are short. Its fur, which varies in colour from brown to grey is more or less speckled with black spots.

Similar species *The racoon.*

Habitat and territory The racoon dog lives in deciduous forests, interspersed with areas of dense vegetation, open land and wet zones at altitudes of less than 600 m. Its home range averages 3 ha. The territories overlap frequently but there is much tolerance between individuals. The nest, where the births take place, and the den, where the dog sleeps through the winter, are found in haystacks, piles of stone or wood, hollow trees, or in burrows, in which the dog cohabits frequently with the fox and the badger.

Food The food of the racoon dog is very varied. Adapted to the available resources depending on season and region, the diet is composed mainly of small prey and vegetation − insects, earthworms, frogs, small birds and rodents, maize and fruits.

Reproduction Mating takes place at the end of winter. The female gives birth in April or May to a litter of 3–8 young (average 4). The species is different from other mammals in the great care which the male takes in feeding and teaching the young, which reach adult size in six months. The basic social group is the family, consisting of the male, female and the young.

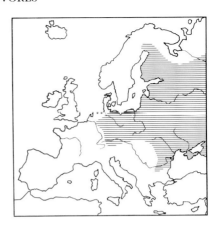

The racoon dog.

PRINTS: each foot has four digits. The imprints of the forefeet are a little larger than those of the hindfeet: 5 x 4.5 cm for the former and 4.5 x 3.5 for the latter. The claws leave marks often allowing them to be distinguished from the cat.

The arrangement of the digital pads makes them easy to distinguish from the fox but they may be confused with those of a small dog (see section on the fox).

DROPPINGS: twisted, they measure 5–8 cm long and 1 cm wide.

TRACES AND OBSERVATION

Indications of presence
TUNNELS: distinguished from those of the fox by a narrow entry trail, less than 20 cm broad, and by a fan–shaped heap of soil in front of the opening to the burrow. In the fox the trail is 25 cm to 30 cm wide and the heap of soil is round.

> **Risks of confusion** *With the prints of a small dog and the faeces of a large mustelid, fox and wild cat.*

Observation The racoon dog is colonising western Europe but it is rarely seen. However its presence can be detected in spring not far from its nest and burrow, and also near water where it hunts amphibians.

The racoon dog.

THE RACOON
Procyon lotor

FAMILY PROCYONIDAE

ECOLOGY AND BIOLOGY

Distribution A native of North America, the racoon has been introduced to Europe where its population is increasing. It is present in East and West Germany, and near the borders with Denmark and Poland. In France it has been reported in the northeast in particular in the Department of Aisne.

Description Total length 60–90 cm of which 20–30 cm are tail; weight 6 kg.

The body of the racoon is heavy and its muzzle pointed. The legs are short and there are black and white rings around the tail which is tufted. The facial mask is black and can cause confusion with the racoon dog.

> **Similar species** *The racoon dog.*

Habitat and territory The racoon lives in mixed forests and wetlands and nests in the hollows of trees and rocks.

Food and reproduction Omnivorous, the racoon hunts a variety of small prey — rodents, frogs, fish, crustaceans and insects.

Mating takes place in winter and 3–4 young are born in spring.

TRACES AND OBSERVATION

Observation The footprints of the racoon measure 7–8 cm long by 6.5 cm wide. Each foot is armed with five digits ending in short claws. The faeces are cylindrical and not tapered at the two extremities.

The racoon is nocturnal. It can be seen at the edge of rivers and lakes where it hunts snails and fish. It climbs trees where it nests.

> **Risks of confusion** With the prints of the otter, the badger and the racoon dog, and with the droppings of the fox, mink and racoon dog.

The racoon.

The brown bear.

The racoon; a new addition to the European fauna.

THE BROWN BEAR
Ursus arctos

FAMILY URSIDAE

ECOLOGY AND BIOLOGY

Distribution Now considerably restricted. The most important populations are in Russia, in the Balkans (Rumania, Yugoslavia, Hungary) and in Scandinavia. Small isolated populations can also be found in northwest Spain and in Italy. About 20 individuals are thought to be present in the French Pyrenees.

Habitat and territory The brown bear inhabits lowland and highland forests. In areas where the population is severely reduced the species is only found in inaccessible mountain areas. If food is sufficiently abundant several individuals may live together in the same area.

Food and reproduction The brown bear is omnivorous and in normal conditions prefers vegetation and fruit, which make up 70–80% of its diet. It

The brown bear.

Description Total length 1.50–2.50 m of which 10 cm are tail; weight of male 90–350 kg, of the female 70–250 kg.

The pelage is uniformly brown and is more or less dark. It cannot be confused with any other European species.

may also consume small and large, wild or domesticated animals.

The mating season is from May to June; young are born in January or February in the den where the female hibernates. The litter consists of 1–3 young, exceptionally 4.

Indications of presence

NEST: the bear makes a cup shaped bed 70–100 cm in diameter and about 10 cm deep. The winter lairs, occupied from December to March are found in rock caves and diverse shelters, or in holes dug by the animal.

PRINTS: the prints of the brown bear are very large measuring up to 25 cm long by 8–15 cm wide. The claws often leave marks 4–8 cm long. The scratches left on trees are made up of three or four parallel marks.

DROPPINGS: usually soft and greenish in spring. In contrast, they form short separate compact buttons in summer and autumn, and the colour varies from violet to yellow depending on the food eaten.

Observation In eastern countries the bear can be seen feeding at artificial baiting stations. Otherwise observation is difficult.

A brown bear footprint.

RODENTS

THE RED SQUIRREL
Sciurus vulgaris

FAMILY SCIURIDAE

ECOLOGY AND BIOLOGY

Distribution: This species is found throughout most of Europe. It has become rare in southern England and is absent from southern Spain and the Mediterranean islands.

Description Total length 35–45 cm, of which 15–20 cm are tail; weight 230–480 g.

The general shape of this squirrel is familiar with its clear brownish to red pelage and with whitish underside. Some individuals are darker. The ears are well developed, and are surmounted by a tuft of long hairs, especially in winter. The eyes are large in proportion to the head. The tail is nearly as long as the head and body. There are four digits on the forefeet and five on the hindfeet, all of which are armed with claws.

> **Similar species** *It can be confused with the fat dormouse although this species is nocturnal and smaller.*

Habitat and territory A forest species, the red squirrel is found wherever sufficient cover is present. It lives in both coniferous and deciduous woods, up to altitudes of 1800–2000 m and can also be seen in parks and gardens, even close to towns. In the forests it prefers areas with a dense shrub layer.

Mostly solitary, but often in pairs, the red squirrel is occasionally seen in groups. Its range is usually 2–4 ha but this area can vary considerably depending on the available food resources.

The red squirrel.

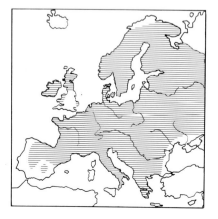

Food The red squirrel is mainly a seed eater, eating conifer seeds and dry fruits found in the forest. It also eats berries, mushrooms, young shoots, buds, bark and sometimes even eggs and nestling birds. As this animal does not hibernate it makes winter stores which are hidden in the ground.

Reproduction If the food supply is sufficient and the climate favourable the breeding season may commence in December continuing through until July or August. The mating behaviour of the male is spectacular, pursuing the female along the branches of the trees. The gestation period is 38 days and 2–5 young are born in each litter. Some females can give birth to two litters each year.

TRACES AND OBSERVATION

Indications of presence
NEST: usually there are several nests in each territory but only one is used in winter and for raising the young. The red squirrel may enlarge the nest of a magpie or a crow or construct its own shelter. It is always high in a tree. The nest measures up to 50 cm in diameter and is composed of small branches and leaves on the outside, and mosses and leaves on the inside. A recent, or inhabited nest can be recognised by the green mosses visible on the outside.
PRINTS: the red squirrel often descends to the ground and tracks can be found in the soil or snow. The gait is bounding and the prints are grouped; the hindfeet, which are longer and have

five digits make prints in front of those of the forefeet which are narrower and have four digits. Each group of prints, measuring 3.5–5.5 cm, are grouped in a trapezium – broader in front than behind – spaced at 60–150 cm apart and going from tree to tree, a characteristic feature of squirrels. In winter the animal may be spotted as it travels, by the small lumps of snow falling from branches.

REMAINS OF FOOD: The remains of meals are frequently seen in the forest when squirrels are present. They may consist of clear patches on the trunks of trees, barked over large areas, or branches without buds. Most frequently pine cones or other cones are found which on close examination are found to have been stripped, with scales remaining only at the pointed end. The work seems a little crude as the scales are not all cut at the same level. Cones may be found clustered together particularly under a branch where the animal regularly eats after gathering the cones. If one looks carefully one can find the uneatable and uneaten remains of seeds – the husk and the wing. The fruit of hazelnuts are cut into two almost equal parts. There are a few traces of teeth marks and a small groove on the side attacked. Young squirrels make deeper grooves to open the hazelnuts.

> ***Risks of confusion*** *With the remains of food left by other small rodents that eat cones although the latter leave them more neatly. Uneaten scales are less frequently seen and these are more regularly cut. The hazelnuts are opened by a regular groove on one side and tooth marks are more apparent. Birds that eat cone seeds open the scales without breaking them.*

Observation The red squirrel can be easily seen in parks or gardens. They may even nest under the eaves of houses, making observation even easier. The animal is common in areas of trees along rivers where the shrub layer is abundant and rich in food. When a favourite feeding place is found feeding can be observed. On some spring and summer days family groups of squirrels travel rapidly through the trees calling with a deep sound. Throughout the period of breeding and raising the young they can be seen close to the nest. If one lives near a forest or woodland it is easy to see the animals and attract them with nuts and hazel nuts regularly given at the same place.

The squirrel at its eating site decorticating a pine cone.

THE GREY SQUIRREL
Sciurus carolinensis

FAMILY SCIURIDAE

ECOLOGY AND BIOLOGY

Distribution A native of North America, the grey squirrel was introduced into several European countries, including Great Britain and Ireland, in the second half of the nineteenth century and the start of the twentieth. Absent from France.

Description Total length 43–52 cm of which 20–24 cm are tail; weight about 500 g.

1 The alpine marmot.
2 The grey squirrel.

Although slightly larger than the red squirrel, the grey squirrel is very similar. The ears are more rounded and never have tufts, giving the head a different appearance.

> **Similar species** *The red squirrel.*

Habitat and territory This species is less dependent on conifers than the red squirrel, and inhabits larger territories – about 5–10 ha for males.

Food and reproduction Similar to the red squirrel.

TRACES AND OBSERVATION

Indications of presence It is only in Great Britain that both species are found and possible confusion arises. The traces left by the two species are very similar. The nest of the grey squirrel is larger than that of the red but the remains of food are alike.

> **Risks of confusion** *With the traces left by the red squirrel (nests, remains of food and tracks).*

Observation In the south of England it is the only squirrel found in gardens and parks. The reduction in population of the red squirrel in the 1940s is due more to a modification of the habitat than competition with the grey squirrel. However, it is possible that the presence of the American species prevents the indigenous squirrel returning to its former habitats.

RELATED SPECIES

The flying squirrel
Pteromys volans

In the forests of Finland and Russia, as in Asia, this small nocturnal squirrel nests in the holes in trees abandoned by woodpeckers. A membrane links the wrist with the ankle allowing this species to plane between trees. It is clearly smaller than the red squirrel.

In 1986, an Asiatic squirrel colonising the Cap d'Antibes was reported. It was probably the red bellied squirrel *(Callosciurus flavimanus)* which is native to Vietnam and Laos. The Siberian chipmunk *(Tamias sibiricus)* a squirrel native to Korea, has colonised much of the Siberian forests and is found regularly in parks and towns. Introduced as a pet into Europe it was allowed to escape. It is easily identified by its striped pelage, with five longitudinal stripes on the back.

THE ALPINE MARMOT
Marmota marmota

Family Sciuridae

ECOLOGY AND BIOLOGY

Distribution The marmot is found in the Jura mountains, in the western alpine arc and in the Tatra mountains (Czechoslovakia). It was introduced to the Pyrenees during 1948 and the Central Massif during 1964 and into certain calcareous alpine ranges – Grand Chartreuse, Vercors.

Description Total length 57–90 cm of which 13–20 cm are tail; weight 4.5–7 kg in autumn, 2.8–3.3 kg in spring.

A large terrestrial squirrel, the marmot cannot be confused with any other animal in its mountain habitat. Of rounded form with relatively short legs and small ears almost hidden in the fur, it has a characteristic appearance. The fur is brown–grey but may appear to be various colours because the hairs have four successive coloured rings. The young are more grey than the adults.

Habitat and territory A mountain species, the Alpine marmot is usually found between altitudes of 1200 and 2700 m. In some valleys it descends to 800 m (Isere) and has reached 3200 m in the Swiss Alps. It seeks the sun. It also frequents the grasslands and the rocky screes under trees, and exposed south facing slopes. Mixed terrain of herbs, bushes and rocks suits it best.

The marmots live in small colonies composed of several females and usually one adult male, in a territory defended against neighbouring groups. In its range, which may extend to 2.5 km², the family finds food and shelter.

Food Mostly herbivorous, the Alpine marmot supplements its diet by capturing invertebrates such as worms,

The marmot enjoys sunbathing on rocks.

beetles and snails. It is even possible to see the animal turning cow pats on alpine pastures to find small prey. However the basic diet consists of foliage, twigs, fruits, grain, bulbs, roots, tubers and the numerous summer mountain plants. It does not store food.

Reproduction Mating occurs above ground, soon after the beginning of spring, in April, and may be accompanied by fighting as the males are very territorial. The gestation period is 34 days, the average number of young in a litter is 3–4. The young remain in the parental territory for two years.

TRACES AND OBSERVATION

Indications of presence In mountainous areas the sharp, short whistle of the marmot is often heard before the animal is seen. It seems that the most developed defensive sense is hearing and not sight.

NEST: in a flat green field the entrance to the burrow can often be seen from a distance – the cone of displaced earth appears distinctly on the grass. In rocks it is less easy to discover. An inhabited burrow shows signs of activity – fresh diggings, flattened grass or droppings. It is often possible to see a group of young at the entrance to the burrow. Underground the tunnels may measure more than 10 m long, with an average diameter of 14–18 cm. The chambers are rarely terminal, except in a winter burrow which is deeper and more complex than the summer burrow. In spring heaps of debris from the winter nest appear in front of the burrow including earth and vegetation.

TRAILS: in densely inhabited areas the trails are easy to see as runs dug in the vegetation and soil, linking the important places such as the principal burrow, secondary shelters and areas for rest and feeding.

PRINTS: when in doubt about the inhabitant of a tunnel examine the footprints on the spoil heap – the marmot has four digits on the forefeet and five on the hindfeet. The prints measure 5 x 4 cm. The digital pads are evenly spaced around the plantar pad.

Risks of confusion *With the tunnels of the fox and the badger, although these are found in the open.*

Observation Being diurnal and large the marmot is easy to see. It is sufficient to sit still and use binoculars. From early spring (end of March, beginning of April) until the entry into the winter tunnels (end of September, beginning of October) there will be numerous opportunities to observe the animals. At the appropriate seasons the raising of the young and the preparation of the winter tunnels can be seen. The marmot's day is divided between a morning feeding period, resting time, social activities and management and digging of tunnels, and a final eating period in the evening. The most striking observation of the marmot is when it sits up to survey its domain, its alarm calls alert observers, even the most inattentive, to its presence.

In emergencies the fat dormouse moves its young.

THE FAT DORMOUSE
Glis glis

FAMILY GLIRIDAE

ECOLOGY AND BIOLOGY

Distribution The fat dormouse inhabits most of Europe but avoids the western maritime region (North Sea, Channel and Atlantic Ocean). It is absent from Scandinavia. In Spain it is not found south of the Cantabrian mountains and has a very restricted distribution in England where it was introduced.

Description Total length 23–37 cm, of which 10–17 cm are tail; weight 70–200 g.

Resembling a small squirrel, but with smaller ears that lack tufts, large eyes with a lighter circle of hair around the eyes, a whitish underside and a well tufted tail.

> **Similar species** *The garden dormouse and squirrels.*

Habitat and territory A forest species, the fat dormouse is found in wooded areas, parks, gardens and may even enter areas of human habitation. It also likes rocks and can live in dry stone walls. The family territory (including a pair or small group) can measure up to 200 m in diameter. The species is found up to altitudes of 1500 m in the Alps and 2000 m in the Pyrenees.

Food Although mainly herbivorous, the fat dormouse will also eat small animals (invertebrates and small vertebrates). It accumulates fat for the winter and also makes food stores.

Reproduction The breeding season begins at the start of spring (April–May). The gestation period is one month and the single litter has 4–5 young. It appears that not all females reproduce each year.

TRACES AND OBSERVATION

Indications of presence A very secretive animal, but can be spotted in the breeding season in spring. At that time it becomes noisy (cries and whistles). It also makes itself obvious when it enters houses in the autumn to store fruits (apples in particular) in a cellar before hibernating.

In the field it is necessary to search amongst the hedgerows and chestnut groves. In mountains it can often be seen on slopes facing the sun. The nest can be found in a hollow tree or in an old wall where a stone is missing, and consists of a mass of moss and leaves. Several individuals may share the same diurnal nest.

> **Risk of confusion** *With the nest of the garden dormouse (the nest of the squirrel is much larger and almost always built in a tree).*

The fat dormouse.

Observation If a nest is found, it should be watched in the evening to see the dormouse emerge. They seem to be very home–loving. Strictly nocturnal, they move easily through vegetation at various heights, often near the ground. In a house the animal is easy to watch especially if attracted by apples. Hibernation may last five to six months – from October to April.

THE GARDEN DORMOUSE
Eliomys quercinus

FAMILY GLIRIDAE

ECOLOGY AND BIOLOGY

Distribution The garden dormouse inhabits the Iberian peninsula, France and Italy. It is also present, in the western Mediterranean islands and in most of eastern Europe. It is absent from Great Britain, Ireland, Scandinavia and the Baltic area.

Description Total length 20–30 cm of which 9 13 cm are tail; weight 50–150 g.

The garden dormouse is easily recognised by its grey back and white underside, and especially by its characteristic head with large eyes and well developed ears which are linked by a very obvious black mask. Its tail is entirely covered by fur and ends in a black and white brush.

Many garden dormice have broken tails. The skin can detach itself, denuding the posterior vertebrae; bleeding is minimal, and the vertebrae dry out and detach leaving only a stump. This is probably a defence mechanism against predation. Other glirids have the same device.

> **Similar species** *The fat dormouse.*

Habitat and territory The garden dormouse is found in woods, parks and gardens as well as rocky areas and house walls. It is found up to altitudes of 2000 m in mountainous areas. Relatively territorial, each individual or group occupies an area of about 150 m diameter, which it defends against other groups. Home–loving, the garden dormouse occupies the same territory from one year to the next. The rat is a serious threat to the dormouse especially in Corsica.

The garden dormouse is easy to recognise by its black face mask.

Food The garden dormouse is amongst the most carnivorous of the European rodents. Depending on the region and season the diet consists of up to 80 per cent animal prey – mostly insects. It will also eat eggs, nestlings, other small invertebrates and vertebrates. The vegetable material eaten includes fruit, seeds and bark.

Reproduction The female garden dormouse normally has only one litter a year except in Corsica where two litters are sometimes born. Mating takes place in early spring – in April – although the males become active a little earlier. The gestation period is about three weeks and the average number of young in a litter is four. Young are born throughout the summer, and reach sexual maturity after the first winter.

TRACES AND OBSERVATION

Indications of presence This species will live near man, especially during hibernation, and during its preparation may leave traces within houses.

NEST: the dormouse may find shelter in a rearranged bird nest, or in a gap between two stones on a cliff filled with moss and vegetation. Holes in trees are also used. The animal can also build a globular nest of moss, resembling that of the squirrel. The summer nest is usually found above ground, several metres up in a tree or a wall. In winter the dormouse chooses a niche – an abandoned box, or a pile of blankets in a cupboard. If not it uses a well protected nest often underground. The animal seems able to tolerate, without difficulty, the glass wool insulating a roof.

PRINTS: the most characteristic traces of the dormouse are often the teeth marks discovered on apples in the cellar of a house. A nest in a blanket, or in similar material also leaves marks. The animal may cut the fabric into pieces to make its hibernation nest more comfortable.

DROPPINGS: like most arboreal species the dormouse does not use droppings to mark its territory. They are rarely found.

> **Risks of confusion** *The nest of the dormouse is similar to that of a small squirrel. In a wall it can be confused with that of the fat dormouse.*

Observation The garden dormouse is the most territorial of the dormice. It can be found as often on the ground as in trees or on a wall, sometimes quite high. Nocturnal, like the other two species, it rarely emerges before dusk. In movement it is usually noisy but is agile, elegant and active. If a nest is found one can wait quietly for the animal to emerge and begin its night activity.

After laying down fat reserves, the dormouse begins its hibernation in October which lasts until April. The males go to sleep first, followed by the females and then the young. Several dormice may be found in a single winter nest.

RELATED SPECIES

The forest dormouse
Dryomys nitedula

A forest species of central and eastern Europe, it is similar to a small garden dormouse, with a black mask around the eyes, but has smaller ears, a greyer pelage and a uniform tail without the black and white tuft.

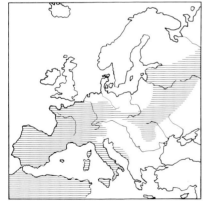

The garden dormouse.

THE HAZEL DORMOUSE
Muscardinus avellanarius

FAMILY GLIRIDAE

ECOLOGY AND BIOLOGY

Distribution Widely distributed in Europe. It extends northwards to the south of England, Wales, and southern Sweden. It is not present south of the Pyrenees. Absent from Corsica but found throughout France. It appears to be more abundant in the east than it once was.

Description Total length 11–16.5 cm of which 5–8 cm are tail; weight 15–35 g.

The hazel dormouse is about the size of a house mouse, but much more thickset. Round in shape, it has a pretty, dense orange fur covering body and tail. Its large black eyes and its round ears make this a very attractive rodent.

Similar species *The harvest mouse and the young garden dormouse.*

Habitat and territory Typically an inhabitant of thickets and brambles, the hazel dormouse lives in the intermediate level of the under shrub layer or the edges of woods. Unlike the fat dormouse and garden dormouse it never enters houses. In mountains it can be found up to 1500 m. The territory occupied is about 150 m in diameter.

Food and reproduction The hazel dormouse lives mainly on buds, with some fleshy or dry fruits, depending on the season, and will not disdain invertebrates.

The breeding season begins after hibernation but most of the nests are built during the summer. The females may have two litters a year, each with 3–4 young, which reach sexual maturity at the end of the first winter.

TRACES AND OBSERVATION

Indications of presence A small arboreal species, the hazel dormouse is mostly discovered because of the nests which it constructs in the shelter of bramble thickets.

NEST: the summer nest is about 6–8 cm in diameter and the breeding nests up to 15 cm in diameter. The hazel dormouse constructs its own nest or rearranges the nest of a bird particularly a wren's, using the material available locally – herbs, leaves and mosses. The summer nests are simply placed in a network of vegetation, between 0.5 and 2.5 m above ground, but are not linked to the vegetation like those of the harvest mouse. The winter nest is found below ground in the hollow of a tree stump, a heap of wood or stones.

TRACES: finely shredded strips of bark from the twigs of honeysuckle indicate the presence of a hazel dormouse. When the animal eats a hazelnut it leaves on the side a characteristic deep groove, the toothmarks appear on the outside but the edge of the hole is perfectly smooth.

Risks of confusion *With the nest of the garden dormouse and the harvest mouse.*

The hazel dormouse.

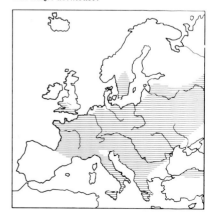

Observation It is the nest of the hazel dormouse that needs to be found. To do this examine the lower parts of brambles and thickets by lying down on your back: the nest will then be seen against a clear background.

Essentially nocturnal, the hazel dormouse is active from sunset in summer but after dusk in winter. It is very secretive in the dense thickets, often only the movement of twigs betrays its passage. If one shakes a bush holding a nest with young they climb rapidly onto nearby branches then stay still.

When the temperature falls below 15–16 °C, in October, the hazel dormouse will generally hibernate and will not awake until April.

A good method for finding places where the hazel dormouse is present is to search, in the autumn after the leaves have fallen, for old nests installed in bushes and brambles. It is sufficient then to return to this area to discover the summer nests which the hazel dormouse will build at the beginning of June, when the vegetation provides dense cover.

THE HARVEST MOUSE
Micromys minutus

FAMILY MURIDAE

ECOLOGY AND BIOLOGY

Distribution The harvest mouse is found throughout central Europe except in Italy and the Iberian peninsula. It is present in most of France except the extreme southwest. It is absent from Corsica.

Description Total length 10–15 mm of which 4–7 mm are tail; weight 4–12 g.

This is the smallest European rodent. The harvest mouse resembles a minute house mouse; its pelage has a yellow–orange colouring contrasting with a white underside. Its ears are small and it has a short muzzle which gives the head a rounded appearance.

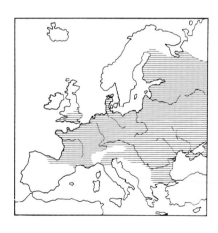

The harvest mouse.

Similar species *Young house mouse, wood mouse and dormouse.*

The hazel dormouse.

Habitat and territory An animal of grasslands, initially adapted to scrub, the harvest mouse also lives in cereal fields and mown grassland and in winter in mills.

Food and reproduction Mostly herbivorous and granivorous, but it can become carnivorous if there is a lack of other food.

From April to September the females can give birth to several litters of 4–6 young. Reproduction seems to be favoured by a damp climate.

TRACES AND OBSERVATION

Indications of presence Very secretive, the harvest mouse leaves few traces except for their spherical nests (about 10 cm in diameter) which are built in brambles, cereals, bushes, and in vegetation on the edges of woodlands. The nests are difficult to find but they are more obvious in autumn when the leaves fall. They resemble balls of dry herbs with one or two lateral openings. Unlike the dormouse the nest of the harvest mouse is strongly linked to the stems of vegetation for support.

> ***Risks of confusion*** *With the nest of the dormouse.*

Observation The harvest mouse is found in plantations of cereals, before the harvest and in the mills in winter. Its winter nest is often found on the ground. Its tail, partly prehensile, permits it to climb the stalks of cereals.

THE HOUSE MOUSE
Mus musculus

ECOLOGY AND BIOLOGY

Distribution Present throughout the whole world, the house mouse has become adapted to all climates and environments even the most extreme. Scientists distinguish a number of species and populations on the basis of morphology and genetics. In western Europe the subspecies *Mus musculus domesticus* is the common species while in eastern Europe it is *Mus musculus musculus*.

Description Total length 12.5–20.5 cm of which 6.5–9.5 cm are tail; weight 10–35 g for the western form.

The grey pelage and the slim silhouette of the house mouse are familiar. The ears and eyes are relatively well developed. The length of the tail is usually equal to, or slightly greater than, the length of the head and body.

The eastern subspecies is more brown and the underside clearly lighter; its tail is shorter than its body.

The house mouse resembles the young wood mouse which is always grey. They can be distinguished by examining the tail which is covered.

The harvest mouse, very agile amongst cereal stalks.

with fine hair (absent in the house mouse) and by the length of the hindfoot (greater than 19 mm, which is the maximum for the house mouse). The profile of the incisor teeth of the house mouse is characteristic. In southern France it is necessary to distinguish this species from the North African species.

> **Similar species** *Young wood mice and the house mouse of North Africa.*

Habitat and territory The astonishing capacity for adaptation shown by the house mouse permits it to occupy habitats as diverse as refrigerated stores, coal heaps and a variety of shelters in the interiors of buildings. It can also live in the open air and so can be found in cultivated areas and in hedgerows. In the north of Europe during the winter it shelters in buildings. In the Mediterranean region it is in competition with the North African species. Being dominant, it relegates the latter to the drier areas and colonises the places where water is available. The house

1 The house mouse.
2 The North African house mouse.

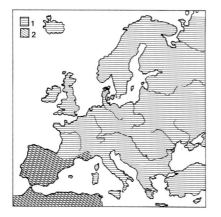

mouse can live for long periods in abandoned villages or old isolated mills.

Food As it is omnivorous, the house mouse eats both animal and vegetable matter. It will also damage inedible materials.

Reproduction Fed and housed by man, the house mouse reproduces throughout the year. In its natural habitat the mating season begins at the time when food is at its most abundant. The social structure is strong, a dominant male mates with several females of the same clan. The gestation period is about three weeks. A female can give birth to 6–10 litters each year.

TRACES AND OBSERVATION

Indications of presence Inside a house, the house mouse is usually secretive. It betrays its presence by leaving its droppings scattered along its routes of activity. The teeth marks are also characteristic.

NEST: although capable of digging its own tunnels, with a resting chamber containing a nest of dry herbs, the house mouse can equally well live in any hiding place. Being so small it is able to squeeze through openings 3 cm in diameter. Old rags and paper which it cuts into tiny pieces make excellent material for the nest.

PRINTS: The tracks left by the house mouse are clearly smaller than those of rats. In natural habitats they are practically impossible to distinguish from the wood mouse. As in the latter the house mouse moves in bounds. In a house, the paths regularly used are often scattered with droppings, urine and dark greasy marks. These paths also have a distinctive and quite strong smell.

DROPPINGS: almost black they are narrow, measuring 6–7 mm in length. Although middens exist where individuals sharing an area leave droppings to mark their territory, the droppings are usually randomly disposed of throughout the area travelled.

Risks of confusion All indications are similar to those of the wood mouse.

Observation In a house it is easy to study the life of a family of house mice because they have regular activities in the course of a day and each day they follow the same paths. The animal is more difficult to see outdoors. However if one remains still after finding a suitable place, one can observe the animals close–up as their eyesight

is poor. As with many small mammals the house mouse is prey for barn owls. In the rejection pellets of this raptor one can discover the remains of skulls which can be distinguished from that of the wood mouse by careful examination of the profile of the upper incisors which are distinctly notched in the house mouse.

RELATED SPECIES

The North African house mouse
Mus spretus

In Europe the North African house mouse, or Lataste's mouse, lives in Spain, the Midi Mediterranean of France and the Balearic Islands. Difficult to distinguish from the house mouse it is a little smaller and has a relatively short tail. It lives exclusively in the wild, not taking advantage of human habitations.

THE WOOD MOUSE
Apodemus sylvaticus

FAMILY MURIDAE

ECOLOGY AND BIOLOGY

Distribution This species is very widely distributed throughout Europe from Iceland to Africa and from the Atlantic to the Altai.

Description Total length 14–22 cm of which 7–10.5 cm are tail; weight 20–30 g.

The wood mouse resembles a large rounded house mouse. It has large black eyes, big ears and a tail lightly covered with fine hairs. The pelage is grey–brown, slightly yellowish, and the underside is whitish. Many specimens have a yellow mark between the forelegs along the median line.

The young, greyer than the adults, are very similar to the house mouse. It is also necessary to distinguish them from the yellow-necked wood mouse, the tail of which is usually longer than the body and there is a complete collar of yellow around the neck.

Similar species *The house mouse and the yellow–necked wood mouse in forests; the field voles in grasslands.*

Habitat and territory The wood mouse is found in nearly every habitat from the plains to the mountains up to 2500 m, from cultivated areas to forests, hedges and gardens. In winter it can be found in houses.

Very mobile, this animal is both a good climber and jumper. It can occupy a range extending for hundreds of metres. It can be found living alongside field and bank voles. The wood mouse is more clearly nocturnal than the voles and there are seldom large numbers of individuals present in an area.

Food The wood mouse prefers cereal grains but will eat a variety of vegetation such as fruits, twigs, buds and bark; its diet may also include some animal prey. It is in turn the prey of several carnivores.

Reproduction Usually the breeding season is limited to the warmer part of the year, but if conditions are favourable the wood mouse can reproduce throughout the year. The gestation period is about three weeks and each litter consists of 3–8 young. The young can reproduce at the age of two months.

TRACES AND OBSERVATION

Indications of presence
NEST: although the entrances appear similar, the tunnels dug by the wood mouse are much deeper than those of

The house mouse, a familiar guest in houses.

voles, but the wood mouse can be found occupying the holes of the voles. In summer the nest is close to the surface, under a plank for example. The remains of meals are often found near the nests — nuts or empty cherry stones, with a hole at one side.

PRINTS: these are difficult to distinguish from those of other small rodents. Inhabiting a range larger than that of a vole it does not use regular paths. The wood mouse moves in bounds, unlike the vole, and their trail in snow resembles a succession of small depressions at the edges of which one can see the trace of the tail.

DROPPINGS: on the ground they are only an aid in indicating its presence.

Observation Rarely seen in groups the wood mouse is one of the most common small mammals. They are crepuscular and nocturnal. They usually frequent places with ground cover. On the ground the wood mouse moves in bounds like a miniature kangaroo, with the tail slightly raised and extended. As a good climber the wood mouse exploits both the bushes and trees to find buds or bark. The long tail helps in balance.

> **Risks of confusion** *With the variety of signs left by the yellow–necked wood mouse, the house mouse and with the tunnels of the field vole.*

The wood mouse can be distinguished from voles by its large ears and long tail.

THE YELLOW-NECKED WOOD MOUSE
Apodemus flavicollis

FAMILY MURIDAE

Distribution Widely distributed in eastern and central Europe. In Scandinavia it is found further north than the wood mouse but it only reaches the south of England and Wales. Rare in Spain and only found in the east of France. Absent from Corsica.

Description Total length 18–26.5 cm of which 9.5–13.5 cm are tail; weight 22–45 g.

In general the yellow–necked wood mouse is heavier than the wood mouse and has a tail at least as long as the head and body. It is difficult to distinguish between the two species. The yellow collar in this species is not always complete but appears transverse as opposed to the longitudinal mark in the wood mouse.

> **Similar species** *The wood mouse.*

Habitat and territory The yellow–necked mouse lives mostly in wooded areas, where it may live in the same habitat as the wood mouse although the reverse is less likely. It is the dominant species of the two. On mountains the species has been recorded up to altitudes of 2000 m.

Food and reproduction Like the wood mouse the yellow–necked wood mouse has a varied diet – both animal and vegetable including the seeds of trees.

It is a much less prolific species than the wood mouse, with a shorter breeding season and fewer young per

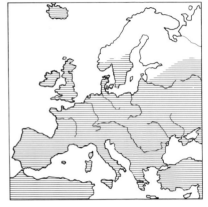

The wood mouse.

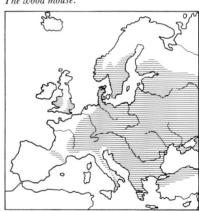

The yellow–necked mouse.

litter. The populations seem to remain stable throughout the year.

TRACES AND OBSERVATION

Indications of presence The traces left by the yellow–necked mouse cannot be distinguished from those of the wood mouse.

> **Risks of confusion** *With the variety of traces left by the wood mouse and the house mouse.*

Observation It is necessary to look in wooded areas. It has a less subterranean life than the wood mouse but its activities are more nocturnal. It climbs high in trees and moves with agility. It is also a good jumper.

THE BLACK RAT
Rattus rattus

Family Muridae

ECOLOGY AND BIOLOGY

Distribution The black rat is found throughout the world, carried by boats from country to country. It is common in the Mediterranean area where the only permanent wild European populations live. It is frequently found in Corsica and the Mediterranean islands.

Description Total length 32–50 cm of which 18–26 cm are tail; weight 140–250g.

Lighter than the brown rat it is also distinguished by the larger ears and eyes and the tail, which is usually longer than the head and body length – although some individuals have the end of the tail missing. The pelage is longer and more shiny than the brown rat and is usually black though pale brown individuals do occur.

> **Similar species** *The brown rat.*

Habitat and territory Although the black rat prefers dry warm places it does not normally live inside houses, but it does inhabit grain stores. This species is a facile climber and wild populations colonise the Mediterranean vegetation where they may meet the dormouse.

Food The black rat is more herbivorous than the brown rat, but it will often destroy bird nests. On some islands it may also feed on small mammals that cross its path.

Reproduction Similar to that of the brown rat; seasonal in its natural habitat, continuous when fed and sheltered by man. On islands where predators are absent it nests on the ground otherwise it makes its nests in trees.

The black rat.

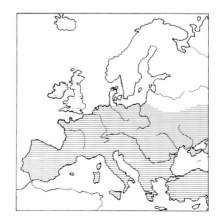

TRACES AND OBSERVATION

Indications of presence The dropp-ings of the black rat, about 9 mm long on average and rounded at the ends, are a little smaller than those of the brown rat. The tracks left by the two species are almost identical but the pathways are less frequently seen and less well marked than those of the brown rat. The nest in a tree may be similar to that of the squirrel.

> **Risks of confusion** *The tracks resemble those of the brown rat and the aerial nest is similar to that of the squirrel.*

Observation This species has been present for a long time in Europe, but since the arrival of the brown rat in the eighteenth century its numbers have declined. The black rat is found main-ly in the Mediterranean and especially the ports. It is very secretive and not easy to see. Occasionally it can be seen walking on the branches of trees.

THE BROWN RAT
Rattus norvegicus

Family Muridae

ECOLOGY AND BIOLOGY

Distribution The brown rat has a world–wide distribution having fol-lowed man wherever he travelled especially by sea. It is therefore found throughout Europe. This species is less well adapted to the Mediter-ranean climate than the black rat and is relatively more frequent in the north.

Description Total length 37–50 cm of which 17–23 cm are tail; weight 250–550 g.

The brown rat is typically rat shaped. The pelage is brown–grey, slightly lighter below, and appears rough. Ears and eyes are not par-ticularly well developed compared to those of the black rat. The length of the hairless tail is always less than the head and body length in contrast to the proportions of the black rat.

> **Similar species** *The black rat, the water vole and the muskrat.*

Habitat and territory · Associated with the presence of man, the brown rat is found in a variety of habitats. It often lives in sewers, caves and damp underground basements. In summer in where the climate is suitable it may live outdoors all the year round. It seeks out bodies of water and digs its tunnels in the banks. It is a good swim-mer.

Domestic rubbish contributes to the success of the brown rat.

The brown rat exhibits territorial behaviour and the hierarchy in a clan is rigid and efficacious. The males are dominant and chase the young from the territory before they reach sexual maturity

Food The brown rat is almost omnivorous and this unspecialised diet has contributed to its success. It can cause serious damage, through soiling and rendering food unfit for human consumption, or by attacking, with the aid of its powerful incisors, many substances; it is capable of penetrating almost any kind of barrier, floor, wall, or piping, to take up residence if it wishes.

Reproduction The fecundity is a reflection of the territory that it occupies and the available food resources. If these are sufficient males and females can breed all year round. The gestation period is 22–24 days at the end of which 6–10 young are born. The females can give birth to 4–5 litters each year.

TRACES AND OBSERVATION

Indications of presence One can look for traces in many places: sewers, food warehouses, and also along river banks or even at the coast.

NEST: a floor (even cement) pierced by an irregular hole 5 cm in diameter or less signals the presence of the rat. On an embankment alongside a canal it is neccessary to differentiate between the holes of the rat and those of the water rat (water vole). The brown rat is larger and its holes therefore are more obvious, the diameter of which may reach 10 cm. The entrances are frequently situated under a shelter of roots or stones.

PRINTS: the feet of the brown rat (4 digits on the forefeet, 5 on the hindfeet) make tracks on a variety of surfaces – soft ground and wet mud at the edge of rivers, dust in stores, or flour spilt on the floor of a bakery etc. The hind footprint, longer than the forefoot can reach 4 cm in length – the upper limit for the footprint of the black rat. The water vole has smaller feet and its digits are a little more star–shaped in particular the forefeet. The track measures only 2.5–3 cm. The tail of the brown and black rats usually make a mark between the footprints, unlike the water vole. The tracks of the brown rat are very clear and regular along its trails, which are about 5–10 cm wide. In a building, where its fur regularly scrapes on a surface there is often a brown greasy mark.

DROPPINGS: measuring on average 1.5 cm long the droppings of the brown rat are small black dull cylinders, which are more tapered at the ends than those of the black rat and more rounded. They are usually grouped. The black rat scatters its droppings throughout its pathways.

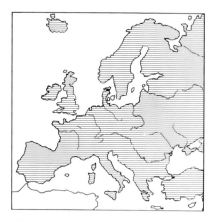

The brown rat.

> **Risks of confusion** *With the tracks of the water vole and the droppings of the muskrat, the black rat and the water vole.*

Observation To look for the brown rat at the bottom of a sewer may appear less pleasant and satisfying than to follow a colony of marmots in the Alps! However the study of this species, which is so difficult to surprise, is interesting.

The brown rat is readily seen at the edge of rivers, close to towns and in various unused places. Mainly active in the morning and evening, it can be seen searching for food amongst all possible food detritus. In fact the individuals most active during the day are immature animals. The dominant animals hunt after nightfall. In rural areas at the side of a stream it is possible to distinguish between the brown rat and the water vole as they swim. Both species can dive but the shape of the brown rat is slimmer than that of the water vole.

THE NORTHERN WATER VOLE
Arvicola terrestris

FAMILY ARVICOLIDAE

ECOLOGY AND BIOLOGY

Distribution Found throughout Europe, except Ireland and Greece. Absent from parts of western France but found from the Pyrenees to the Cantabrian mountains in Spain, the only area of the Iberian peninsula where it is found.

Description Total length 19–33 cm of which 7–11 cm are tail; weight 80–250 g. The water vole resembles a

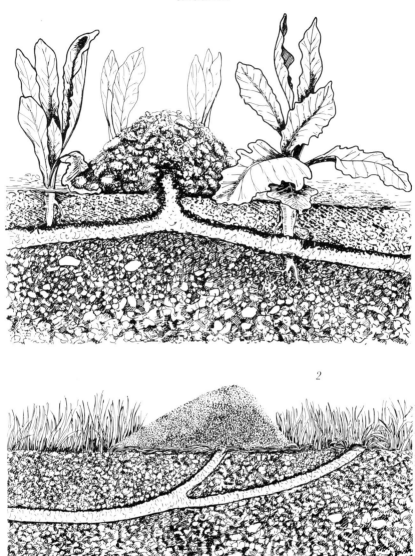

Sections through the molehills of: 1 the mole; 2 the water vole.

giant pine vole. Usually brown in colour, its pelage varies from almost black to light yellow. Its eyes and ears are small, a common feature in burrowing animals.

Similar species *The southwestern water vole, the muskrat and the brown rat.*

Habitat and territory There are two recognised subspecies of water vole living in different habitats. *A. t. sherman* is the terrestrial form and *A. t. terrestris* is the more aquatic form. The latter closely resembles the southwestern water vole. It lives exclusively at low altitudes. The terrestrial form is found in open habitats from 200 m to an altitude of more than 2000 m. It is commonly found in cool wet grasslands. The animals dig tunnels on two levels: the first superficial and the second deep (down to 1 m), and they seldom emerge from the tunnels.

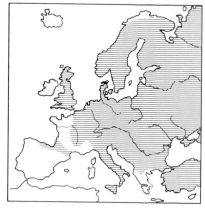

The northern water vole.

The northern water vole.

The tunnels of the southwestern water vole can be found at times of low water.

Food The water vole eats both the aerial and underground parts of vegetation. It will also eat cultivated plants and tree roots.

Reproduction From spring to autumn the female water vole can have three to four litters of 4–5 young after a gestation period of three weeks. When conditions are favourable the population may reach plague proportions with hundreds of individuals to the hectare, causing severe local damage to crops.

TRACES AND OBSERVATION

Indications of presence

NEST: the 'molehills' are the most obvious sign of the presence of water voles. They differ from those of moles by the fine texture of the earth which is a result of the water vole using its teeth to dig rather than its feet. Also the opening of the tunnel is oblique instead of vertical.

PRINTS: these are seldom found. The aquatic form leaves a trail similar to the southwestern water vole on the silt of the water course where it lives.

DROPPINGS: small green–black cylinders measuring 5–8 cm long. They are similar to the droppings of other herbivorous rodents. They are rarely found on the surface.

> **Risks of confusion:** *the 'molehills' are similar to those of the mole. Each species can live in the tunnels of the other. The prints and droppings of the aquatic form are like those of the southwestern water vole (though the two species seldom live together) and those of the brown rat.*

Observation: The species is subterranean and nocturnal (especially in winter) and therefore difficult to see. It may appear above ground more often during the day in summer.

THE SOUTHWESTERN WATER VOLE
Arvicola sapidus

FAMILY ARVICOLIDAE

ECOLOGY AND BIOLOGY

Distribution This species has only recently been distinguished from the northern water vole. It is limited to the Iberian peninsula and the greater part of France, although it is absent from the north and northeastern departments. It is also absent from Corsica.

Description Total length 28–35.5 cm of which 11–13.5 cm are tail; weight 150–280 g.

The southwestern water vole has the rounded vole shape. Its ears are hidden in the brown–grey pelage which is slightly lighter and yellowish below. It is slightly smaller, slightly lighter in colour and has a relatively longer tail than the northern species. They can be distinguished by examination of the skulls. Both species can be aquatic.

> **Similar species** *The northern water vole, the muskrat and the brown rat.*

Habitat and territory The southwestern water vole lives close to rivers and ditches that are regularly flooded. It prefers slow flowing streams with densely vegetated banks. It can be found in lowlands, but is also present up to 1500 m in the Alps and 2000 m in the Pyrenees. The species is relatively diurnal and active throughout the day. Social activity is more intense early in the morning and in the evening.

Food Herbivorous, the southwestern water vole feeds on a great variety of terrestrial vegetation. Occasionally it will eat invertebrates, frogs and fish.

Reproduction The breeding season begins in March or April and continues until October. Males and females chase each other in the water, emitting small cries and mating takes place close to the edge of the water or even in it. The gestation period is three weeks. Litters average 6 young.

underwater entrance on the bed of the stream. In marshy terrain where there are no suitable banks the vole will make its nest in the tufts of grass above water. Lifting the nest will reveal a mass of finely cut grass from which a network of galleries radiates.

The tunnels of the southwestern water vole contain a nest of dry grass. Alongside these tunnels are others, open at both ends running under a stone, where the animal can hide, dry itself or simply rest. The animal modifies its nest as and when neccessary, opening and closing the entrances.

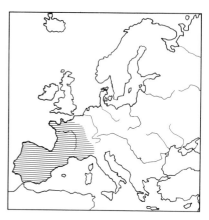

The southwestern water vole.

TRACES AND OBSERVATION

Indications of presence

NEST: the southwestern water vole digs a tunnel in the banks of a river. Some tunnels open under water, others above. In clear calm waters a small heap of spoil can be seen outside the

PRINTS: the traces made by the southwestern water vole are smaller than those of the brown rat: 2.5 cm for the hindfeet as against 3.5–4 cm in the rat. The tail does not make a mark. As well as the prints it is possible to see the trenches made by the animals as they leave the water regularly at the same spot. These trenches lead under the grass on the bank to the places where the animal feeds. They are strewn with the white hearts of twigs cut by the voles, as only the green exterior parts of reeds seem to be eaten.

DROPPINGS: these are small and cylindrical about 5–8 cm long, of very fine texture and more rounded at the ends than those of the brown rat with which they might be confused. They are deposited regularly in obvious places – on emergent stones, on the pathways and in the tunnels and sometimes in small heaps.

> **Risks of confusion** *With the nests of the water shrew and the muskrat. The droppings are similar to those of the brown rat and the muskrat.*

Observation The animal is often active by day and it is possible to observe them by keeping still. However they can be more easily approached in the early morning and in the evening when the light is less strong. When swimming on the surface it shows most of its back whilst the brown rat swims submerged with only its muzzle showing and seems to have to make great efforts to maintain even this position. When the vole dives in clear water it can be seen walking on the bottom or swimming vigorously using its hind-legs. With the pelage pressed to the body it is much more hydrodynamic than its general shape suggests.

THE COMMON VOLE
Microtus arvalis

FAMILY ARVICOLIDAE

ECOLOGY AND BIOLOGY

Distribution The common vole is widely distributed in Europe but is absent from the Great Britain (except the Orkney Islands) and Scandinavia in the north and from the Mediterranean zones in the south. In the Alps between 1400 and 3000 m altitude another species *Microtus incertus* is found.

Description Total length 12–17 cm of which 3–4.5 cm are tail; weight 18–40 g.

The common vole has a rounded shape and very small eyes. The tail is short and the ears partly covered by the brown pelage, which is a little lighter below.

> **Similar species** *All the other voles.*

Habitat and territory The common vole lives in open country – on grasslands, arable land (legumes and

The common vole.

cereals), polders and embankments. Usually it avoids areas with trees. Each individual has a small territory, perhaps less than 10 m in diameter if the available food is adequate. Within this range several holes lead to a tunnel system with a nest of grass.

This species is particularly common in grasslands and crops and may often be the most abundant species in suitable localities. It is the principal prey of many carnivores, both mammals and birds.

Food Almost exclusively vegetarian, the common vole eats many cultivated plants (trefoil, lucerne, etc.) as well as many of the wild plants of banks and grasslands. It can also eat insects. When present in large numbers the animal is capable of rapidly destroying a crop. They can occasionally be seen feeding sitting up on their haunches lifting their food to the mouth using the forefeet.

Reproduction Highly prolific, the field vole can reproduce before the age of two months. The gestation period lasts about 20 days and if conditions are good, births take place every three weeks. Fewer births take place between October and February.

TRACES AND OBSERVATION

Indications of presence

NEST: grassland or fields inhabited by the common vole are sprinkled with small holes 3–4 cm in diameter indicating the presence of the animals. By pouring plaster down the holes, the shape of the tunnel system can be studied. Several tunnels 2.5 cm in diameter lead to a chamber lined with dry grass. This may be only 20 cm below ground. The total length of the tunnels is about 1–2 m. In winter, when the temperature falls below 0°C, the inhabited tunnels are easily recognised. The humidity produced by the

The road network dug by voles in grasslands.

respiration of the animals condenses in contact with the cold air and deposits small crystals of ice around the opening.

PRINTS: the tiny prints left by the common vole are difficult to find. This also applies to all the small voles. However, between the tunnels and tufts of grass where the entrances to tunnels are sometimes hidden, narrow pathways

The common vole.

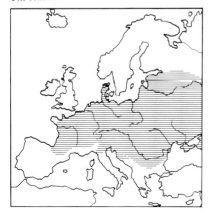

may be seen, especially in snow, leading from one hole to the next. Sometimes the voles can be seen moving along these paths.

DROPPINGS: the common vole usually deposits its droppings in a particular place forming a 'toilet', which can be recognised as a space devoid of vegetation where the small black and greenish, cylindrical pellets, 3–4 mm long, accumulate. Often there is a pathway from the 'toilet' to the nearest hole.

> **Risks of confusion** *With the signs of presence of other species of* Microtus, Pitymys, *and* Clethrionomys *which are almost identical.*

Observation This species is often active during the day and lives a more subterranean life than the field vole. It is fairly easy to observe depending on the density of the population. In a wheat field after the harvest, if the straw is left on the ground, the voles may be very numerous but seldom seen. A network of tunnels and a nest may be found under a sheet of metal or a plank of wood which has lain on the ground for a few weeks. One indirect way of establishing the presence of the animal is by examining the rejection pellets of nocturnal raptors.

Depending upon which other voles may be present in the neighbourhood the common vole may occupy all the available space or be limited to certain areas. For example the common vole and the common pine vole confine their close relative to the dryer grassy zones, whilst the snow vole keeps them out of rocky areas.

RELATED SPECIES

The root vole
Microtus oeconomus

Widely distributed in northern Europe, the root vole is similar to the field vole and seems to be well adapted to wet habitats. An isolated population lives in the Low Countries and another in central Europe.

THE SNOW VOLE
Microtus nivalis

FAMILY ARVICOLIDAE

ECOLOGY AND BIOLOGY

Distribution A mountain species, the snow vole has a very discontinuous distribution in Europe – mountain range to mountain range, from Spain to Asia minor.

Description Total length 14–21 cm of which 4.5–7 cm are tail; weight 30–65 g.

It is the largest of the small voles, it has a clear grey pelage and a longish tail. The large vibrissae (bristles) are a characteristic feature.

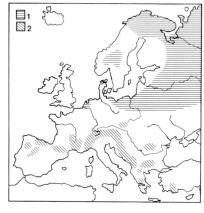

1 The root vole.
2 The snow vole.

Habitat and territory Mainly an animal of rocky habitats. On mountains the snow vole frequents the exposed screes up to 3000 m as well as the hills of the Mediterranean region and low altitudes in suitable places.

> **Similar species** *The other voles, especially the field vole.*

Food and reproduction The food of the snow vole is exclusively vegetable except when it occurs near mountain chalets.

The species is less prolifc than the other voles. The litters are smaller and fewer in number, but they appear to live longer. This may be linked to the stable environment the animal prefers.

found. Droppings, beginnings of tunnels, a nest of dry herbs or a small store of food under stones may indicate the presence of this animal.

> **Risks of confusion** *Few problems on mountains.*

Observation Locally abundant. The snow vole is diurnal and can be seen without difficulty near the screes where it lives. It is necessary to stay very still. By turning over stones some traces may be discovered, or even the animal itself, as it does not dig the soil to any great extent.

TRACES AND OBSERVATION

Indications of presence The snow vole leaves few traces on the rocky screes. At altitude it is the only vole

THE FIELD VOLE
Microtus agrestis

FAMILY ARVICOLIDAE

ECOLOGY AND BIOLOGY

Distribution The distribution of this species is similar to that of the common vole except that it is also found in Great Britain and in Scandinavia. It also inhabits the northern and western shore of the Iberian peninsula.

Description Total length 11–18 cm of which 2.5–4.5 cm are tail; weight 18–60 g.

Slightly larger than the common vole these two species are difficult to distinguish between. The pelage is brown

above and grey below and is a little rough in texture. The ears are hidden in the fur. The best character to separate the two species is the surface feature of the second upper molar.

> **Similar species** *The common vole.*

Habitat and territory The field vole avoids places where the ground is too open, like polders, but can be found in areas with light cover in hedgerows, fields, orchards and open forest. The preferred areas are more humid than those frequented by the common vole. Found on mountains up to altitudes of 2000 m.

Food and reproduction Similar to that of the common vole. However the bark of trees is frequently found in the diet. Reproduction is identical to that of the common vole.

Observation The various species of voles are seen under the same conditions and there is usually only one species present in a given locality. The population density of the voles may be unstable and can vary from 1–2 individuals to the hectare to several hundred.

TRACES AND OBSERVATION

Indications of presence As with the common vole the field vole makes runs in the vegetation, which are scattered with small droppings that are green and oval when fresh containing small pieces of cut vegetation. The runs lead to the openings of underground tunnels.

Risks of confusion *With the variety of signs left by other small voles.*

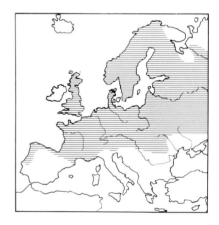

The field vole.

THE BANK VOLE
Clethrionomys glareolus

FAMILY ARVICOLIDAE

ECOLOGY AND BIOLOGY

Distribution Widely distributed in Europe, the bank vole is absent from the extreme north of Scandinavia and from the Mediterranean countries. It is present throughout France except on the southeast coast and in Corsica.

Description Total length 10–19 cm of which 3–6.5 cm are tail; weight 15–30 g.

The back of the bank vole is much more red than that of other species. The grey colour on the flanks and underside is also characteristic. It has the longest tail of any of the small voles except for the snow vole.

Similar species *The other voles.*

The bank vole.

Habitat and territory The bank vole lives in forests and thickets and all wooded habitats up to an altitude of 2000 m. It is also found in agricultural areas.

Food and reproduction This rodent eats both vegetable and animal food.

It is precocious and can reproduce almost all year round. The gestation period is a little less than three weeks.

TRACES AND OBSERVATION

Indications of presence
The bank vole digs tunnels just below the surface of the soil, at a depth of 2–10 cm. The nest can be either underground or above ground in a bush.

Food remains accumulate in the tunnels. The hazelnuts eaten by this species have a large circular hole surrounded by clear tooth marks.

The droppings are often deposited in heaps and are narrower than those of the wood mouse (one quarter of their length) and less green than those of the field vole. In winter the voles move below the snow on the surface of the soil in order to attack the bark at the base of trees. The marks then become visible in spring.

> ***Risks of confusion*** *With the other small rodents which leave similar traces, especially tooth marks. The droppings are also difficult to identify.*

Observation

Although usually nocturnal the bank vole sometimes emerges by day. As it seems not to be shy it can be watched if the observer stays still. It moves on the ground or climbs in trees and bushes with great agility. It can also jump. This species is more sociable than other voles and can sometimes be seen in groups of several individuals. The populations fluctuate in numbers but not as widely as in some other voles. The characteristic tufts of red hair found in the droppings of carnivores and in the rejection pellets of raptors

similar life to that of the bank vole although adapted to the colder weather.

The Norway lemming
Lemmus lemmus

The Norway lemming looks like a large vole but it has a very short tail and its pelage is vividly coloured in black, yellow and orange. It inhabits the treeless areas of Scandinavia and its numbers fluctuate in a cyclical manner every 2–4 years.

1 The wood lemming.
2 The Norway lemming.

The bank vole.

indicate the presence of bank voles in the area.

The wood lemming
Myopus shisticolor

The wood lemming is about the size of a bank vole but it has a very short tail. Its distribution stretches from Scandinavia to Asia. Linked to coniferous forests, this species does not fluctuate in numbers like the Norway lemming.

RELATED SPECIES

The grey–sided vole *(C. rufocanus)* and **the northern red–backed vole** *(C. rutilis)* which inhabit the north of Europe and Asia and live a very

THE COMMON PINE VOLE
Pitymys subterraneus

FAMILY ARVICOLIDAE

ECOLOGY AND BIOLOGY

Distribution The common pine vole occupies a wide area of Europe, in a band extending from Brittany to Russia. It is absent from the north and south of the continent.

Description Total length 10.5–16.5 cm of which 2.5–4 cm are tail; weight 14–25g.

Thickset and with a short tail, the common pine vole is very small. Its pelage is relatively dark and a little rough. It has small eyes and resembles a field vole. The external characters of this species do not allow differentiation from other species of *Pitymys*.

1 The Mediterranean pine vole.
2 The Pyrenean pine vole.

Habitat and territory The habitat of the pine vole overlaps that of the field and common voles although the three species do not cohabit. It is found in open spaces, open woodlands as well as gardens and parks, and bogs.

Food and reproduction The common pine vole is mainly herbivorous.

The pattern of reproduction is similar to that of the field vole.

TRACES AND OBSERVATION

Indications of presence It lives a more subterranean life than the field vole but leaves comparable traces. It sometimes seals the entrances of its tunnels during periods of rain or ice. Remains of the species are occasionally found in the rejection pellets of raptors which suggests that the animal spends time above ground.

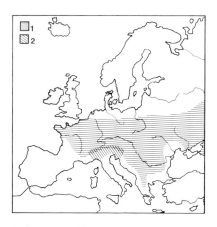

1 The common pine vole.
2 The alpine pine vole.

Similar species *All other pine voles.*

> **Risks of confusion** With other voles.

Observation Mainly nocturnal, but the animal will emerge during the day. It can feed below ground which does not make direct observation easy.

RELATED SPECIES

The alpine pine vole
Pitymys multiplex

The alpine pine vole, or Fatio's pine vole, inhabits the alpine arc between the Rhone in the west and Yugoslavia to the east. It is not possible from its morphology to distinguish this species from the common pine vole or the alpine vole *Microtus incertus*. These

species never cohabit. Savi's pine vole *(Pitymys savii)*, another related species, is present in the Alps Maritimes.

The Mediterranean pine vole
Pitymys duodecimostatus

The Mediterranean pine vole is found through much of Spain and the south of France as well as in the Dordogne, and north of Lyon. It replaces *Microtus arvalis* and *M. agrestis* on the Provencale coast. *Pitymys lusitanicus*, the Lusitanian pine vole is found in the more humid southwest. The species are impossible to separate on morphological characters.

The Pyrenean pine vole
Pitymys pyrenaicus

This species is found throughout southwestern France and in the extreme north of Spain. It can co–exist with *Microtus arvalis*, *Pitymys subterraneus*, *P. lusitanicus* and *P. duodecimostatus*.

THE COMMON HAMSTER
Cricetus cricetus

FAMILY CRICETIDAE

ECOLOGY AND BIOLOGY

Distribution A species of the steppes of central Europe.

Description Total length 25–34 cm of which 3–6 cm are tail; weight 150–500 g.

The stocky shape, very short tail and tricoloured pelage – it is black

underneath – make the hamster easy to recognise.

Habitat and territory The hamster avoids wet habitats. A solitary species with each individual inhabiting its own subterranean burrow which it defends against its relatives.

Food and reproduction Herbivorous and seed–eating, the hamster is renowned for the way it stores food underground for the winter. It transports the food in its cheek pouches and

The common hamster.

can accumulate several kilograms of seeds, tubers, roots, etc. In a good season, it may eat invertebrates (mainly insects) and small vertebrates.

The breeding season occurs at the end of spring and beginning of summer.

TRACES AND OBSERVATION

Indications of presence The distribution limits the possibilities of seeing this animal in Europe. It hibernates from October to April, closing the entrances to its burrows. The end of hibernation is signalled by the opening of the holes and fresh debris outside the entrances at the end of March. The openings measure 5–7 cm in diameter. The hamster does not make a molehill in contrast to the large voles and avoid the grasslands inhabited by this species.

> **Risks of confusion** *The tunnels resemble those of several burrowing rodents.*

Observation The species is often nocturnal but may emerge during the day, when it may be possible to see it. To appreciate its ability to tunnel one must dig to a depth of 2 m, and a radius of about 10 m.

THE MUSKRAT
Ondatra zibethicus

FAMILY CRICETIDAE

ECOLOGY AND BIOLOGY

Distribution A native of North America. The animal was introduced into Europe (Czechoslovakia) in 1905. The first commercial fur farms were established in France in 1920–1930, in Alsace, the Ardennes and in Normandy. As farms were abandoned there were accidental escapes and deliberate introductions, and the muskrat has now colonised all France and most of northern Europe.

Description Total length up to 65 cm of which 20–25 cm are tail; weight 1.5 kg.
   The fur of the muskrat – brown like the whiskers – is dark on the back and light underneath. The mammae are ventral. The tail is a characteristic feature and is laterally flattened.

The muskrat is much larger than the water vole and smaller than the coypu and the beaver.

> **Similar species** *The coypu and the beaver.*

Habitat and territory This species is found in almost all wet areas, for example ponds, lakes, rivers, canals and marshes, where there is abundant aquatic vegetation .

Food The muskrat eats all types of aquatic plants, reeds, rushes, water lilies, etc. In winter it eats mainly roots, which it seeks underwater. In summer it prefers the vegetation of river banks and cereal crops in which it can do serious damage. It also eats vegetables, the bark of young trees and even though rarely, fish and aquatic molluscs.

Reproduction The muskrat is very prolific: the female can give birth to

The common hamster.

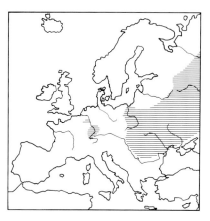

The muskrat.

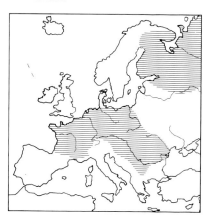

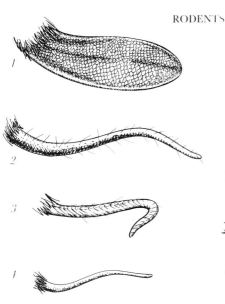

These mammals can be identified by comparing their tails: 1 the beaver; 2 the coypu; 3 the muskrat; 4 the brown rat.

2–3 litters each year with 6–8 young in each. The breeding season lasts from March to October depending on the climatic conditions. The gestation period is about 30 days and the young are born in the burrows, reaching independence by the autumn. The young born later may spend the winter with their parents. A pair of muskrats can increase their numbers by tenfold in a season. When food is abundant the density can reach 70 animals per hectare.

Footprints of the muskrat in mud.

TRACES AND OBSERVATION

Indications of presence

BURROWS: burrows are usually occupied only during the breeding season but may be used all year round if the animals are living far from stretches of water. They consist of several chambers and a network of tunnels, which may extend for several dozen metres under the banks. The entrance measures 15–25 cm in diameter, is usually situated under water and usually has a run clearly visible in clear shallow water. The tail of the muskrat leaves a trail in soft mud.

HUTS: the muskrat builds heaps of vegetation for the winter shelter. It begins the task in September–October and can continue to improve the structure until February–March, when these habitations will be deserted. The muskrat uses all available materials – twigs, branches, leaves and even mud. The heap varies between 1.5 and 2 m in diameter at the base and its height above water may be 0.5–1.6 m. The underwater entrance gives access to 1–2 chambers which can accommodate up to eight individuals. The accumulated vegetation is used for insulation and not for food.

PRINTS: These resemble stars, the five claws extending the digits. The prints of the forefeet measure 3.5 x 3 cm and those of the hindfeet, longer because of the heel, 7 x 5 cm. Usually only 3 digits of the forefeet make marks.

RUNS AND DROPPINGS: the runs seen in vegetation on river banks are 20–30 cm wide. They are frequented by many other animals. The runs of the muskrat can be recognised by the droppings which it leaves, often in small heaps, at the entrances and exits of the runs. Droppings are also left on various projections and raised places – heaps of earth, tufts of reeds, trunks of trees, stones sticking out of the banks.

The droppings of the muskrat resemble an olive stone. They vary in colour from green to black. Measuring 1–1.5 cm long by 0.5 cm wide. Sometimes they are smaller and may be confused with water vole droppings.

> **Risks of confusion** *With the droppings left by the water rat and the coypu, and with the prints of the otter, the badger, the racoon and the coypu.*

A muskrat roadway in a marsh.

Observation The muskrat is one of the easiest animals to see. It is active all year round, and often in daytime. The best time for observation is at dusk. In order to see them it is enough to remain still at the edge of a pond, canal or river with calm water where they live. Most often they can be seen swimming. The best seasons for observation are in the summer when they emerge to feed on corn (they cut the stalks about 25 cm from the ground) and in the autumn when they are building their heaps for the winter.

The heap of a muskrat at the edge of the water.

THE COYPU
Myocastor coypus

FAMILY CAPROMYIDAE

ECOLOGY AND BIOLOGY

Distribution A native of South America where it is known as nutria. It was introduced to France in 1882, and in other European countries at the start of the twentieth century. In the 1930s it was raised for fur, but through being abandoned and from negligence they were allowed to escape and colonise areas of England and France. Small colonies are widely distributed in other European countries of western Europe including Scandinavia.

The commercial exploitation of the coypu under the name of Chilean

The coypu.

beaver, or marsh beaver caused much confusion with real beaver.

Description Total length 0.70–1.05 m of which 30–45 cm are tail; weight 6–10 kg.

The pelage of the coypu is dark brown above lighter brown below. The vibrissae are white and the mammae dorso–lateral which allows the young to suckle in the water. Round and cylindrical the tail is scaly and has a scattering of stiff hairs. This is the best character to distinguish it from the muskrat, in which the tail is laterally flattened and the beaver which has a wide flat tail resembling a bat.

> **Similar species** *The muskrat, the beaver and the otter.*

Habitat and territory The coypu lives in all wet areas, but is present especially in marshes, at the edges of canals, ponds and slow flowing rivers. The distribution is very fragmented because the animal cannot survive very rigorous winters, it is not found in mountain areas nor in the northern regions. Its spread is thus limited by altitude and by the availability of suitable water networks.

A family occupies a territory of about 1.5 ha, more or less depending on the available food resources. Females with young are less wide ranging than males.

Food Similar to the food of the muskrat. Mostly aquatic vegetation, grasses, tender bark and cereals. It causes serious damage to crops, notably in maize where it cuts the stems at a height of about 60 cm, three times higher than the muskrat which adopts the same strategy to get at the grain.

The coypu often gathers food on platforms to strip it and these heaps of food remains can be readily seen.

Reproduction Mating takes place at any time of year although it is most frequent at the end of winter and in the autumn. After 130 days gestation the female gives birth to 2–3 young. There may be two litters each year. The young begin to disperse at the age of three months.

DROPPINGS: these are found where the coypu emerges from the water or near places where it eats, and are relatively easy to recognise. The general shape is that of a small gerkin or a banana, red or brown in colour. They measure 3–4 cm long by 1 cm wide. When the droppings are fresh they appear longitudinally striated.

> **Risks of confusion** *With the prints left by the muskrat, the beaver and the otter.*

TRACES AND OBSERVATION

Indications of presence

BURROWS AND PATHWAYS: the coypu does not build a hut in contrast to the muskrat or beaver. It lives all year round in a blind burrow 2–3 m deep. The entrance, measuring 50 cm in diameter, is situated under water or is semi–submerged. In front of the entrance there is a visible trench, the result of repeated use. The runs or pathways are similar to those of the muskrat, but larger, 30 cm and more, but those of the coypu and the muskrat often appear similar.

PRINTS: the general shape of the prints, although larger, are similar to those of the muskrat. The five evenly spaced digits are lengthened by long claws. The forefeet measure 5.5 x 3.3 cm and the hindfeet, with the heel, 11 x 8 cm The forefoot has pads on four digits only and in most cases the palm leaves no trace and only the base of the digits and the claw marks are visible.

Observation The coypu is easy to see even without a hide, by waiting patiently at the edge of the water. It is active throughout the year and emerges at dusk and during the day. The best technique for seeing them is to slowly scan the edges of the water with binoculars. One can see the ripples on the water and soon they can be seen swimming. The best times of year to watch the coypu are during the harvest in summer and during spells of intense prolonged cold. When short of food the animals will emerge. In hard winters feeble individuals can be seen walking on the banks or on the ice.

The coypu.

The tracks in mud betray the presence of the coypu.

The characteristic dropping of a coypu.

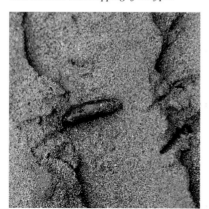

THE EUROPEAN BEAVER
Castor fiber

FAMILY CASTORIDAE

ECOLOGY AND BIOLOGY

Distribution Nowadays the European beaver inhabits only a fraction of its natural range. Its disappearance from Europe (and Asia) is largely due to hunting for its excellent fur. In many places the animals found are the result of reintroductions.

Description Total length 1–1.3 m of which 25–40 cm are tail; weight 12–40kg.

The European beaver.

The beaver is the largest rodent of the northern hemisphere. Its shape, like a fat marmot, is characteristic. Its tail, flat and scaly, is unique amongst European mammals. An amphibious animal, it shows marked adaptations to life in water; small eyes and ears, nose placed high on the muzzle, webbed feet and a very dense pelage.

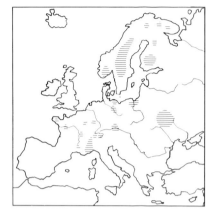

The European beaver.

Similar species *The Canadian beaver (Castor canadensis), (introduced), the coypu (introduced), and the otter.*

Habitat and territory The beaver lives in freshwater, running or stagnant, which does not totally freeze in winter nor dry up in summer. The ideal stretch of water is 1–2 m deep. In the Rhône valley the beaver survives in dead branches of the river, where it finds shelter and food. It prefers the banks of stretches of water lined by willows, poplars and birch, on which it feeds. The animal seldom ventures more than 20–30 m from water, and its territory, which it marks with secretions from a gland called a castoreum, forms a narrow ribbon along the course of the water.

Food Exclusively herbivorous, the beaver eats branches and the bark of trees, usually poplars and willows. It also eats ash, aspen, alder, etc. and fruit trees planted near water. The beaver stores food for the winter, gathering tree branches which are stored below water.

Reproduction: The beaver lives in family groups with a single adult pair. The adults are paired for several years, if not for life. The female dominates the other members of the group including the male. The young up to two years of age form part of the family. Mating takes place, in the water, between December and April. Gestation lasts 100–128 days and each litter has about four young. In the Canadian species the litter size may be up to eight young.

TRACES AND OBSERVATION

Indications of presence The current distribution of the European beaver is very fragmented and corresponds mainly to recent well known sites of reintroduction. Research allows us to follow the maintenance and development of colonies.

NESTS: although the presence of beavers is associated with large huts

206

Section of a beaver hut, which can reach 15 m in diameter and several metres in height.

and dams, in Europe the animal is much more discreet. The beavers living along the Rhône valley live in burrows rather than huts. However since the species has been protected some more spectacular constructions have appeared.

The burrows have an entrance and a ventilation hole. This holds true whether the home is surrounded by water or attached to the bank. The base is always a foundation of gathered branches. The roof consists of vegetation (branches and leaves) and some wood shavings are used to line the interior. The whole construction is very large.

PRINTS: the hindfoot prints of the beaver are large (15 cm long by 10 cm wide) and those of the forefeet are 3.5 x 4.5 cm. The first two digits make less clear marks than the remaining digits. The tail leaves a wide trace. The animal also makes canals approaching trees which it intends to cut

down and which it attacks in a characteristic fashion – gnawing the trunk to the shape of a pencil point. The trunks cut measure on average 20 cm in diameter.

DROPPINGS: usually invisible as the beaver tends to defecate in water. The pellets are small, light, dry and odourless and rapidly dispersed.

> ***Risks of confusion*** *The webbed feet leave footprints in mud which are similar to those of the coypu. The broad trace left by the tail is quite different. When the animal is in water the nose of the coypu, the otter and the muskrat can be confused. The clap of the tail which the beaver uses as an alarm signal is characteristic.*

A tree wounded and barked by a beaver.

Observation In Europe, the places where the beaver lives are well known. To observe it it is neccessary to get into position near the family home. Beavers are crepuscular and nocturnal. They are less active in winter. If the water is clear they can be seen swimming. They are capable of staying under water for 15 minutes. If they are seen feeding on land they are very shy.

The droppings of a beaver (above) composed of vegetable fibres and those of a fox (below).

THE LESSER MOLERAT
Microspalax leucodon

FAMILY SPALACIDAE

ECOLOGY AND BIOLOGY

This animal is well adapted to the subterranean life in the steppes. It weighs about 200 g. Cylindrical in shape, its eyes are non–functional and the animal does not have ears or a tail. It lives in the southeast of Europe (the Balkans and shores of the Black Sea). Also called the western molerat.

RELATED SPECIES

Podlie's molerat
Spalax polonicus

Recently distinguished from the greater molerat *(Spalax micropthalmus)* this species lives in southeastern Poland and the southwest of Russia.

THE PORCUPINE
Hystrix cristata

FAMILY HYSTRICIDAE

ECOLOGY AND BIOLOGY

A large rodent of characteristic shape, the porcupine is an African species, that was introduced to southern Italy and Sicily a long time ago. It is nocturnal and very secretive, and passes the day at the bottom of a burrow which it digs itself. In Europe its numbers are declining.

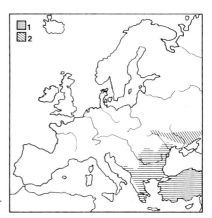

1 The lesser molerat.
2 The greater molerat.

THE BROWN HARE
Lepus capensis

FAMILY LEPORIDAE

ECOLOGY AND BIOLOGY

Distribution The brown hare is found over a large part of Europe but is absent from Ireland (except for local introductions) and from much of Scandinavia where the variable hare is common.

Description Total length 50–73 cm of which 7–11 cm are tail; weight 3–5 kg.

Its large size, large black–tipped ears, which are longer than the head, and the elongated hindfeet distinguish the brown hare from the rabbit. Its silhouette is also more elongated. The brown–red pelage mixed with white and black provide good camouflage in the field. The underside is white and the tail has a black upperside and white underside.

Similar species *The rabbit and the variable hare.*

Habitat and territory Although colonising almost all the habitats in Europe with the exception of the alpine zones and coniferous forests, the hare shows a preference for temperate open habitats. It is found on grasslands, scrub, sometimes in broadleaved woods and particularly on cultivated land. On mountains it is present up to altitudes of 2000 m and can co–exist with the variable hare.

An adult occupies a territory of about 300 ha which it shares with

The brown hare.

Tracks made in mud by: 1 the rabbit; 2 the hare.

other individuals. Depending on circumstances it may use only part of its range, from 10–20 ha, which it changes regularly.

Food The brown hare is a herbivore eating a variety of wild or cultivated plants. It feeds for only short periods at each place, and leaves few traces of its presence, in contrast to the rabbit which appears more destructive. However it leaves its traces when it attacks the bark of young trees during the winter. In a bad season, hares will eat animal corpses. Like the rabbit it produces soft pellets during the night, rich in nutrients, which it eats immediately. In this way it recovers extra proteins and vitamins from its digestive system.

Reproduction In the brown hare the reproductive season lasts from the beginning of the year until the autumn. The behaviour of a male around a female in season is always very animated. Gestation lasts six weeks and the female can mate again immediately after giving birth. There are 2–4 litters a year with 3–5 young in each. They are born with their eyes open, have bodies covered with hair and are in a much more advanced state of development than the rabbit.

may also find shelter in a bush or in thickets in woods. The nest of a hare can be found by following tracks or by detecting droppings left nearby. Where the nest is found depends on the season, the weather, and the food resources around.

PRINTS: clearly larger than those of the rabbit, and very characteristic. The hindfeet leave parallel marks and show five digits when the ground is soft, whilst the forefeet make angled prints leaving a cylindrical mark, with only 4 digits. The hare moves in bounds leaving a series of prints in general forming a Y – the two forefeet, one behind the other, then the two hindfeet, parallel and in front of the forefeet. In effect the hare brings its hindfeet forward before bounding.

DROPPINGS: The droppings of the hare are round and measure 1–2 cm in diameter. They are difficult to distinguish from those of the rabbit. In general they are paler and of a more fibrous consistency.

> **Risks of confusion** *The tracks of the brown hare are difficult to separate from those of the variable or mountain hare. The droppings are easily confused with those of the variable hare and the rabbit.*

TRACES AND OBSERVATION

Indications of presence

NEST: although the hare neither tunnels nor lives in burrows, it has a number of nests in its territory. They are usually a simple depression in a dry ditch or between two furrows. It

Observation In a region of mixed cultivation with hedges and small woods it should be possible to see hares. At all seasons they can provide an interesting spectacle. In spring when the vegetation is low, they can easily be seen performing the antics that preceed mating, provided one maintains a reasonable distance. Habitually crepuscular, the hare may also be active early in the morning and the afternoon. In the middle of the day it rests in a field of grass or in a cornfield. The places where it hides can easily be found.

If surprised, the hare may first lie low on the ground, relying on camouflage before taking flight. Its rapid running is punctuated with leaps but it is less bounding than that of a rabbit.

The trail of a hare in snow. The footprints form a Y.

THE VARIABLE HARE
Lepus timidus

FAMILY LEPORIDAE

ECOLOGY AND BIOLOGY

Distribution The variable hare or mountain hare inhabits the alpine arc and Scandinavia. It is also present in Scotland and in Ireland where it is the only indigenous hare present. It is found in the French Alps and was introduced between 1978 and 1982 into the Pyrenees, close to the Pic d'Anie.

The variable hare may have a pure white coat in winter.

Description Total length 48–70 cm of which 4–8 cm are tail; weight 2–3 kg.

Smaller than the brown hare, this species has a more rounded form, shorter legs, and the length of the ears does not exceed that of the head. The pelage is grey–blue in summer and white in winter. Only the tips of the ears remain black.

Habitat and territory A mountain species, the variable hare inhabits areas between altitudes of 1300 and 3000 m. Thanks to the snow and the

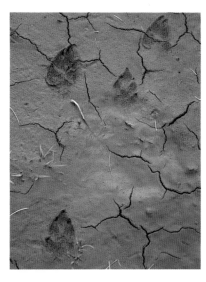

The tracks of a bounding hare in mud.

tracks left in it, the hare's winter domain is better known than its summer one. During the winter it lives in a territory about 100 ha in size. The animal prefers, winter and summer, rocky screes and ridges, where it finds both shelter and food.

Food In summer the variable hare eats grasses, legumes, many annual herbs and in winter will eat woody

TRACES AND OBSERVATION

Indications of presence

NEST: in common with the brown hare, this species does not dig burrows. Tolerant of cold, it shelters simply in a crevice at the foot of a rocky ridge or under a juniper bush. In winter the shelters can be found by following the

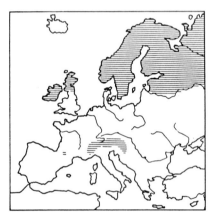

The variable hare.

vegetation: bark, buds, twigs or leaves. In spring it eats soil for which no explanation can be given. Like the brown hare it practises refection (it eats the pellets it produces).

Reproduction The mating season begins in February–March and traces of the mating chases can be seen in the snow. In a season the female may have up to 3 litters with 2–5 young in each. The young are well developed at birth.

Tracks of lagomorphs in snow:
1 the hare; 2 the rabbit.

tracks in the snow. It may stay at one shelter for several days.

PRINTS: very similar to those of the brown hare. In winter the variable hare often uses the tracks left by skiers, particularly those following its normal routes. In summer the brown hare will climb up to 2000 m, and at this time it is practically impossible to distinguish between the tracks of the two species.

DROPPINGS: identical with those of the Brown Hare.

> ***Risks of confusion*** *With the various traces left by the brown hare.*

The rabbit.

Observation On mountains, in the winter, in the snow the tracks of the variable hare are unmistakable because at this time the brown hares have descended to live in the valleys. As the animal is mostly nocturnal it is difficult to observe directly. In summer when the nights are short they can be seen at dawn and dusk when they are most active. This species seems to move long distances in winter to find food. To discover its presence it helps to look in places sheltered from the wind and where the snow melts quickly. As with the brown hare it adapts its pattern of life to local conditions.

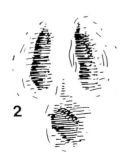

2

THE RABBIT
Oryctolagus cuniculus

FAMILY LEPORIDAE

ECOLOGY AND BIOLOGY

Distribution Once limited to the western Mediterranean basin the rabbit is now present throughout Europe and has been introduced into many other countries.

Description Total length 38–54 cm of which 4–8 cm are tail; weight 1–2 kg.

The rabbit is amongst the best known species. Small, rounded in shape and with grey–brown fur. The long ears are smaller than the head, unlike the hare. The belly and the underside of the tail are white.

It should be noted that individuals affected by myxomatosis have characteristically swollen heads, sometimes described as being 'lion headed'.

> **Similar species** *The common hare and the Florida rabbit.*

Habitat and territory Originating from the warm dry areas of southwest Europe, the rabbit has been introduced to the north along with the disappearance of the great forests. It now inhabits moorland, fallow land, woodland edges, hedgerows, and thickets. It is found in the Alps up to altitudes of 1000 m and in the Pyrenees up to 2000 m. Its range of activity is seldom more than 150-200 m from the bur-

row and lives in a family colony that consists of a male, several females and their young.

Food Herbivorous, the rabbit eats a variety of vegetation, from small plants to shrubs. It appears to prefer cultivated plants like cereals, decorative flowers or young fruit trees. In common with hares, the rabbit produces caecotrophes, the nutritive rich faeces which it resorbs directly.

Reproduction Prolific, the rabbit can reproduce for a large part of the year. Before mating, which usually takes place below ground, the male runs after the female, jumps over her and sprays her with urine. The gestation period is a little less than a month. The female gives birth to 3–5 litters a year each with about 3–7 young. A female can thus raise up to 30 young in a year. The burrow in which young are born is distinct from the large family burrow. It is a small trench with a nest of grass and hair. The female will obstruct the entrance when she leaves the nest. The young are born completely naked, blind and deaf, and their growth is much less rapid than that of young hares.

TRACES AND OBSERVATION

Indications of presence
NESTS: rabbit holes are familiar sights. Some areas, occupied for generations

The entrance to a rabbit hole. ▶

The toilet of a rabbit.

become veritable underground fortresses with many ramifications. They are usually found on an embankment where the ground slopes gently. The holes are often protected by bushes or thickets. There are tunnels in the vegetation, leading to the entrance. The tunnels can descend to 2 m below the surface, the type of soil dictating the degree of burrowing. In stony soil the rabbit is content with the shelter of rocks.

PRINTS: these resemble those of the hare but are smaller. The long hindfeet make marks in front of the forefeet which are much more circular. As the animal hops most of the time and seldom walks its tracks appear as a succession of small depressions 20–30 cm apart. The track is usually somewhat irregular.

REMAINS OF MEALS: found close to the burrow at the edge of fields where the rabbit finds food. When it attacks the bark of trees it does not make long scratches like the squirrel and is not interested in anything except the base of the trees or branches on the ground.

DROPPINGS: small pellets of about 1 cm in diameter, sometimes difficult to distinguish from those of the hare. It often leaves them on a small bump of land near its burrow or sometimes in a small scratched hole.

Risks of confusion *With the prints and the pellets of the hare.*

Observation The rabbit is probably the easiest mammal to observe. It emerges long before dusk and often in the afternoon in spring. The antics of a family of rabbits are a spectacle to delight the observer.

The Florida rabbit.

Rabbit footprints in mud.

THE FLORIDA RABBIT
Sylvilagus floridanus

FAMILY LEPORIDAE

ECOLOGY AND BIOLOGY

Distribution The Florida rabbit inhabits the eastern side of North America, from southern Canada to the south of central America. Recent attempts have been made to introduce it into Italy and the southeast of France but with little success. Little is known of its distribution in France, as all the releases are clandestine.

Description Total length 38–47 cm of which 3–4 cm are tail; weight 0.9–1.8 kg.

The Florida rabbit is reputed to be resistant to myxomatosis.

A small rabbit, round in form, its neck is clearly red and its white tail is highly visible when in flight.

Similar species *The rabbit.*

Habitat and territory In North America the Florida rabbit appears to prefer regions of mixed agriculture, with plantations of hedges and woods. It does not make burrows.

The droppings of the doe are more rounded than those of the stag.

Food and reproduction Herbivorous, the Florida rabbit prefers grasses. Reproduction resembles that of the rabbit.

TRACES AND OBSERVATION

Observation This rabbit has a lifestyle similar to the hare. In the USA it lives together with other species of the genus. It was introduced into France in order to replace the rabbit but authorisation for this has not yet been given.

As this species seems unable to maintain a population in Europe, little is known about the traces that individuals leave in their passage. They probably closely resemble those of the rabbit.

> **Risk of confusion** *With the assemblage of traces left by the rabbit, and the nest of the hare.*

UNGULATES

THE WILD BOAR
Sus scrofa

FAMILY SUIDAE

ECOLOGY AND BIOLOGY

Distribution The wild boar has a vast range – it is found from the Atlantic to the Pacific. In Great Britain it has been extinct for at least two centuries and it is also absent from Scandinavia (except for two small areas in Sweden).

Description Total length 1.1–1.3 m; shoulder height 1 m or more; weight up to 300 kg.

The wild boar cannot be confused with any other species living in Europe. However the black Corsican domestic pig is similar and can hybridise with the wild boar. Some wild boars have been crossed with sows imported from the continent in an attempt to improve their fecundity.

◀ *The traces of a wild boar searching for food.*

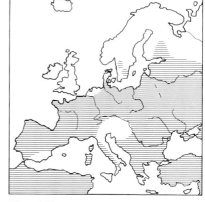

The wild boar.

Habitat and territory It prefers the deciduous and mixed forests but the Mediterranean maquis also seems to suit the species. It seeks wet muddy areas where it likes to wallow.

Food and reproduction The wild boar is an omnivore. Although certain individuals specialise in hunting sheep these are exceptional.

Mating takes place in autumn and winter. The gestation period is similar to the domestic sow – three months, three weeks and three days. The female makes a nest of branches ready to give birth. The piglets are striped.

TRACES AND OBSERVATION

Observation The breeding nest, unique amongst ungulates, can be found in spring. The most characteristic sign of the presence of a wild boar is the track which shows four digits. The two posterior hooves are smaller and more separated than the fore hooves. The prints of the wild boar measure 6–7 cm broad. The anterior part is narrower. The traces of digging, where the boar turns over the earth, or where it has wallowed, and its tracks in the fields of maize are also characteristic. Only domestic pigs raised in the forest will leave similar tracks.

The droppings of the wild boar may resemble small cylinders, 5–7 cm in diameter, but they are usually very irregular.

> **Risks of confusion** *With the prints of the domestic pig, and deer when only the anterior hooves make prints.*

THE RED DEER
Cervus elaphus

FAMILY CERVIDAE

ECOLOGY AND BIOLOGY

Distribution The red deer is found in forests throughout Europe. Its distribution is discontinuous and the animal is usually restricted to larger areas of forest although it can also exist on moorland (in Scotland, for example). Introduced centuries ago to Corsica, it has recently disappeared from the island and attempts are now being made to reintroduce it.

Description Total length 1.6–2.5 m; height at shoulder 1–1.5 m; weight 100–300 kg.

The red deer is the largest of the wild herbivores in Europe. The head has a long profile, its rump is brown

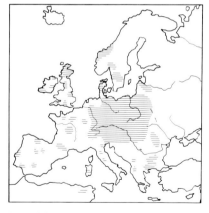

The red deer.

and partly covered by the equally dark tail and a lighter band runs along the back of the thigh.

> **Similar species** *The sika, fallow and roe deer.*

223

Habitat and territory A forest species, the red deer is found in extensive forests and the bordering areas. It is present in mountains up to altitudes of 2500 m.

Food and reproduction The red deer feeds on grasses, twigs, buds, bark, mushrooms, fruit and cultivated plants.

In autumn (at the end of September and beginning of October) during the mating season, the roaring of the stags is one of the most impressive sounds of forest life. The spotted fawn is born 8 months later.

TRACES AND OBSERVATION

Observation The footprints of the red deer are the largest tracks to be found in the forest. They are 8–9 cm long by 6–7 cm wide in the adult male. The points of the digits are often separated and the print is usually wider at the front.

The droppings are black and cylindrical, measuring 1.5 cm in diameter and 2–2.5 cm long. Several elements may adhere together.

During autumn evenings the roaring is a characteristic sound. At the end of the summer one can find trees or saplings against which the deer has frayed its antlers. The small trees are often damaged by the deer.

> **Risks of confusion** *The droppings of the red deer resemble those of other ruminants. The prints are similar to those of the sika and fallow deer but they are larger than those of the roe deer and show two digits, in contrast to those of the wild boar.*

RELATED SPECIES

The sika deer
Cervus nippon

Originating in the Far East (China, Korea, Japan) the sika deer has been relatively recently introduced into Europe. Smaller than the red deer it has a rounder shape and the pelage is quite dark and remains spotted until maturity. The sika and red deer can hybridise.

The fallow deer
Dama dama

Of Mediterranean origin, the fallow deer is essentially a parkland animal but there are a few wild groups scattered throughout Europe. The antlers of the male are characteristic, they become very flattened in the old males. The fallow is smaller than the red deer and the adult pelage remains spotted. White and melanic forms are not uncommon.

The elk
Alces alces

In Europe the elk only inhabits Scandinavia and the Baltic states, as far south as Poland. The shape is characteristic. In the male the antlers are flattened and palmate.

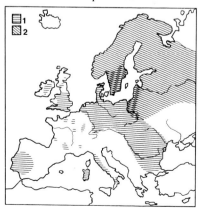

1 The fallow deer.   2 The elk.

A deer hoofprint.

THE ROE DEER
Capreolus capreolus

FAMILY CERVIDAE

ECOLOGY AND BIOLOGY

Distribution The roe deer is widely distributed in Europe but it is absent from Ireland and the Mediterranean islands.

Description Total length 0.9–1.3 m; shoulder height 60–80 cm; weight 15–30 kg.

The roe deer is the smallest European cervid. The muzzle is marked with black whilst its chin and lips are spotted with white. On the rump there is an obvious round white patch.

> **Similar species** *The other species of deer.*

Habitat and territory This species is found in a variety of woodland, open moorland (provided that there is enough deep heather), marshy reed beds and sometimes cultivated areas close to human habitation.

Food and reproduction The roe deer eats mainly the leaves of trees and shrubs but will also eat other vegetation.

It is probably the only ungulate which demonstrates delayed implantation. Mating takes place in July but gestation does not begin until the beginning of the next year and lasts about 5 months. The fawn is spotted.

The roe deer.

TRACES AND OBSERVATION

Observation The tracks of the roe deer resemble those of the red deer although much smaller. The imprint of each hoof measures 4.5 cm long by 3 cm wide. The prints appear more pointed.

The droppings form small cylinders 1.4 cm long by 0.8 cm wide. As in other species the appearance of the droppings varies with the season depending on the food.

During mating the male chases the female and the pair run round and round until a characteristic circular track is formed.

> **Risk of confusion** *With the prints and droppings of the sheep, goat, and sometimes the red deer. The droppings can sometimes be confused with those of the brown hare.*

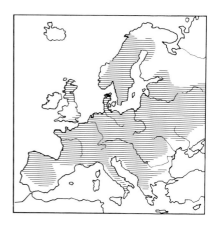

THE MOUFLON
Ovis ammon

FAMILY BOVIDAE

ECOLOGY AND BIOLOGY

Distribution At present all the wild mouflon are descendents of the Corsican and Sardinian mouflon, that are themselves descended from animals introduced to the islands long ago (?Neolithic times), which in turn came from Asia Minor. In France they are found in the Alps, the Massif Central and the Pyrenees.

Description Total length 1.1–1.3 m; height at shoulder 60–80 cm; weight 25–55 kg.

The European mouflon is the smallest mouflon. The pelage is chocolate brown, the male has a white saddle, while in the female the back and flanks are brown. In summer the coat of the mouflon becomes a lighter colour. The horns are small or absent in the female but well developed, curved and ringed in the male. Some individuals are atypical and show the result of hybridisation with domestic sheep.

> **Similar species** *Domestic sheep, the chamois and the ibex.*

Habitat and territory The habitats in Europe are more wooded and less dry than the original natural habitat. It is found at middle altitudes on mountains.

Food and reproduction The mouflon feeds on herbaceous plants and shrubs.

The mouflon.

Mating takes place in autumn, and a single young is born five and a half months later.

TRACES AND OBSERVATION

Observation It is practically impossible to distinguish the tracks of the mouflon from those of domestic sheep which in summer frequent the same pastures. The points of the hooves are clearly separated and the print measures about 6 cm x 4.5 cm.

The droppings of the mouflon are more spherical than cylindrical and measure about 1 cm in diameter. They are difficult to distinguish from those of the roe deer except when left in small heaps like those of sheep.

> **Risks of confusion** *The prints and droppings are practically the same as those left by domesticated sheep and are also difficult to distinguish from those of the roe deer.*

Depending on the terrain and the speed of movement the tracks of the roe deer may appear different.

The droppings of the roe deer are hollowed at one side.

◀ *Only the male roe deer has antlers.*

THE IBEX
Capra ibex

FAMILY BOVIDAE

ECOLOGY AND BIOLOGY

Distribution The systematics of the ibex is somewhat confused. Some authors distinguish between the Alpine ibex *(Capra ibex)* which is limited to the western part of the Alpine arc, and the Pyrenean ibex *(Capra pyrenaica)*, which occurs in the Spanish mountains, from the Asiatic species.

The Alpine ibex inhabits the protected areas of the Alps (Vanoise and Mercantour in particular) whilst the Pyrenean ibex has disappeared from the French side of the range.

Description Total length 1–1.5 m; height at shoulder 0.70–1 m; weight 80–100 kg.

The Alpine ibex is larger than its Pyrenean relative. The big curved horns of the males are a characteristic feature.

> **Similar species** *The domestic goat, the chamois and the mouflon.*

Habitat and territory An animal of rocky cliffs, the ibex is an extraordinary climber but does not seem to be at home in the snow. It is restricted to areas above the tree line but could probably live at much lower levels.

Food and reproduction The ibex eats grasses in summer and lichens in winter.

A single young is born in spring after a gestation of five and a half months.

TRACES AND OBSERVATION

Observation Living mostly in rocky areas, the ibex leaves little trace of its presence. Its very mobile hooves assist it in climbing, but in soft soil the mobility is not apparent in its tracks.

The droppings closely resemble those of the domestic goat. They are

The alpine ibex.

spherical, or slightly cylindrical, measuring about 1 cm in diameter and are always separate.

The animals are not timid and can be easily observed.

> **Risks of confusion** *With the tracks and droppings of the goat and the chamois.*

THE CHAMOIS
Rupicapra rupicapra

FAMILY BOVIDAE

ECOLOGY AND BIOLOGY

Distribution The chamois lives in the Alps, the mountains of the Balkan peninsula, the Carpathians, the Tatras and as far east as the Caucases. The populations in the Abruzzes (Italy) and the Pyrenees belong to another species – (*R. ornata* – the isard). In France the chamois is found in the Jura mountains, the Alps, the Cantal (introduced), the Voges (introduced) and the isard in the Pyrenees.

Description Total length 1–1.4 m; shoulder height 75–85 cm; weight 20–50 kg.

The chamois is larger than the related isard. The black and white

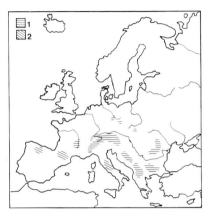

1 *The chamois.*
2 *The isard.*

markings on the head and the small crotchet shaped horns, present in both sexes are a characteristic feature.

> **Similar species** *The ibex, the mouflon, the domestic goat.*

Habitat and territory A mountain species, the chamois descends into the forest in winter and climbs to an altitude of 4000 m in summer.

Food and reproduction Herbivorous, the chamois changes its diet depending on season and availability of food: herbaceous plants, shrubs, lichens.

The mating season is in autumn and a single young is born after more than five months gestation.

TRACES AND OBSERVATION

Observation The tracks are seldom seen except in winter in the snow. Its hooves are less well adapted to the rocky habitat than those of the ibex but it is at ease in snow thanks to the interdigital ligament. The prints measure about 6 cm x 3.5 cm. The hooves are well separated, but are usually parallel.

The droppings of the chamois measure 1.5 cm in diameter and are almost spherical. They resemble those of other ruminants of comparable size such as the sheep. However the droppings of the latter are often left in small piles and each element, pressed against the others, have plane surfaces. Those of the goat have a more regular form.

> **Risks of confusion** *With the droppings of the ibex, however the tracks of the ibex form a 'V' shape.*

Species Index

This index refers to the systematic part of the book.

The numbers in **bold** refer to the pages where the species is described.

The numbers in normal print refer to the pages where the species is mentioned in the text.

The numbers in *italics* refer to the pages where there are illustrations.

FURTHER READING

General Works

BANG, P. AND DAHLSTROM, P. 1974. *Animal tracks and signs*. Collins, London.

BROSSET, A. 1974. *Mammiferes sauvages de France et d'Europe de l'Quest*. Nathan, Paris.

CLARKE, M. 1981. *Mammal watching*. Severn House Publishers Limited, London

CORBET, G., OVENDON, D. AND SAINT-GIRONS, M.C. 1984. *Les mammiferes d'Europe*. Bordas, Paris

CORBET, G.B. AND SOUTHERN, H.N. (EDS.) 1977. *The handbook of British mammals* (2nd Edition). Blackwells, Oxford.

ORR, R. AND POPE, J. 1983. *Mammals of Britain and Europe*. Pelham Books Ltd., London.

LAWRENCE, M. AND BROWN, R. 1973. *Mammals of Britain, their tracks, trails and Signs*. Blanford, London.

MALLINSON, J. 1978. *The shadow of extinction: Europe's threatened wild mammals* Macmillan, London.

Works on particular groups

Hedgehogs

MORRIS, P. AND BERTHOUD, G. 1987. *La Vie du Herrisson*. Delachaux and Niestle, Neuchatel.

STOCKER, L. 1987. *The complete hedgehog*. Chatto and Windus, London

Moles

MELLANBY, K. 1971. *The mole*. Collins, London.

Shrews

CROWCROFT, P. 1957. *The life of the shrew*. Max Reinhart, London.

Bats

HILL, J.E. AND SMITH, J.D. 1984 *Bats – a natural history*. British Museum (Natural History), London.

STEBBINGS, R.E. AND GRIFFITH, F. 1986. *Distribution and status of bats in Europe*. Institute of Terrestrial Ecology, Huntingdon.

YALDEN, D.W. AND MORRIS, P.A. 1975. *The lives of bats*. David and Charles, Newton Abbot.

Lagomorphs

LOCKLEY, R.M. 1976. *The private life of the rabbit*. (2nd edition). Andre Deutsch, London.

Carnivores

BURTON, R. 1979. *Carnivores of Europe*. Batsford, London.

MECH, L.D. 1970. *The wolf*. The Natural History Press for the American Museum of Natural History, New York.

NEAL, E. 1977. *Badgers*. Blanford, Poole.

LAIDLER, L. 1982. *Otters in Britain*. David and Charles, London.

Rodents

GURNELL, J. 1987. *The natural history of squirrels*. Christopher Helm, London.

TWIGG, G.I. 1975. *The brown rat*. David and Charles, Newton Abbot.

Ungulates

WHITEHEAD, G.K. 1964. *The deer of Great Britain and Ireland*. Routledge and Kegan Paul, London.

CHAPLIN, R.E. 1977. *Deer*. Blanford.

CHECKLIST OF SPECIES IN BOOK ORDER

Order Insectivora

Family Erinaceidae
Erinaceus europaeus	Western hedgehog
Erinaceus concolor	Eastern hedgehog
Erinaceus algirus	Algerian hedgehog

Family Talpidae
Talpa europaea	Northern mole
Talpa caeca	Blind mole
Talpa romana	Roman mole
Galemys pyrenaicus	Pyrenean desman

Family Soricidae
Suncus etruscus	Pygmy white-toothed shrew or Etruscan shrew
Neomys fodiens	Water shrew
Neomys anomalus	Miller's water shrew
Sorex araneus	Common shrew
Sorex coronatus	Millet's shrew
Sorex minutus	Pygmy shrew
Sorex alpinus	Alpine shrew

Crocidura russula	Common or Greater white-toothed shrew
Crocidura leucodon	Bicoloured white-toothed shrew
Crocidura suaveolens	Lesser white-toothed shrew

[Note: Corbet includes *Sorex granarius, S. samniticus, S. caecutiens, S. minutissimus, S. sinalis.*]

Order Chiroptera

Family Molossidae
Tadarida teniotis	European free-tailed bat

Family Rhinolophidae
Rhinolophus ferrumequinum	Greater horseshoe bat
Rhinolophus mehelyi	Mehely's horseshoe bat
Rhinolophus blasii	Blasius's horseshoe bat
Rhinolophus euryale	Mediterranean horseshoe bat
Rhinolophus hipposideros	Lesser horseshoe bat

Family Vespertilionidae
Myotis myotis	Greater mouse-eared bat
Myotis daubentoni	Daubenton's bat
Myotis brandti	Brandt's bat
Myotis capaccinii	Long-fingered bat
Myotis dasycneme	Pond bat
Myotis blythi	Lesser mouse-eared bat
Myotis mystacinus	Whiskered bat
Myotis emarginatus	Geoffroy's bat
Myotis nattereri	Natterer's bat
Myotis bechsteini	Bechstein's bat

[Note: Corbet includes *Myotis nathalinae, Lasiurus cinereus and Nycteris thebaica*]

Eptesicus serotinus	Serotine
Vespertilio murinus	Parti-coloured bat
Eptesicus nilsonii	Northern bat
Nyctalus noctula	Noctule
Nyctalus leisleri	Leisler's bat
Nyctalus lasiopterus	Greater noctule
Pipistrellus pipistrellus	Common pipistrelle
Pipistrellus kuhli	Kuhl's pipistrelle
Pipistrellus savii	Savi's pipistrelle
Pipistrellus nathusii	Nathusius's pipistrelle
Barbastella barbastellus	Barbastelle
Plecotus auritus	Common long-eared bat
Plecotus austriacus	Grey long-eared bat
Miniopterus schreibersi	Schreiber's bat

Order Carnivora

Family Mustelidae
Mustela nivalis — Weasel
Mustela erminea — Stoat
Mustela putorius — Western polecat
Mustela eversmanni — Steppe polecat
Vormela peregusna — Marbled polecat
Mustela furo — Domestic ferret
Mustela lutreola — European mink
Mustela vison — American mink
Martes foina — Beech marten
Martes martes — Pine marten
Lutra lutra — Otter
Meles meles — Badger
Gulo gulo — Glutton

Family Viverridae
Genetta genetta — Genet
Herpestes ichneumon — Egyptian mongoose
[Note: Corbet includes *Herpestes edwardsi*]

Family Felidae
Felis silvestris — Wild cat
Felis lynx — Lynx

Family Canidae
Vulpes vulpes — Fox
Alopex lagopus — Arctic fox
Canis lupus — Wolf
Canis aureus — Jackal
Nyctereutes procyonoides — Raccoon dog

Family Procyonidae
Procyon lotor — Raccoon

Family Ursidae
Ursus arctos — Brown bear
[Note: Corbet includes *Thalarctos maritimus*]

Order Rodentia

Family Sciuridae
Sciurus vulgaris — Red squirrel
Sciurus carolinensis — Grey squirrel
Pteromys volans — Flying squirrel
Callosciurus flavimanus — Red bellied squirrel
Tamias sibiricus — Siberian chipmunk
Marmota marmota — Alpine marmot

[Note: Corbet includes *Spermophilus citellus* and *S. suslicus*]

Family Gliridae
Glis glis — Fat dormouse
Eliomys quercinus — Garden dormouse
Dryomys nitedula — Forest dormouse
Muscardinus avellanarius — Hazel dormouse

[Note: Corbet includes *Myomimus roachi*]

Family Muridae
Micromys minutus — Harvest mouse
Mus musculus — House mouse
Mus spretus — North African house mouse or
Algerian mouse

Apodemus sylvaticus — Wood mouse
Apodemus flavicollis — Yellow-necked wood mouse
Rattus rattus — Black rat
Rattus norvegicus — Brown rat

[Note: Corbet includes *Apodemus microps, A. mystacinus, A. agrarius, Mus hortulans, Acomys minous*]

[Note: Corbet also includes the **Family Zapodidae** with *Sicista betulina and S. subtilis*]

Family Arvicolidae
Arvicola terrestris — Northern water vole
Arvicola sapidus — Southwestern water vole
Microtus arvalis — Common vole
Microtus incertus — Alpine vole (see p 144 for mention)
Microtus oeconomus — Root vole
Microtus nivalis — Snow vole
Microtus agrestis — Field vole
Clethrionomys glareolus — Bank vole
Clethrionomys rufocanus — Grey-sided vole
Clethrionomys rutilis — Northern red-backed vole
Lemmus lemmus — Norway lemming
Myopus schisticolor — Wood lemming
Pitymys subterraneus — Common pine vole
Pitymys multiplex — Alpine pine vole
Pitymys savii — Savi's pine vole
Pitymys duodecimostatus — Mediterranean pine vole
Pitymys pyrenaicus — Pyrenean pine vole
Pitymys lusitanicus — Lusitanian pine vole

[Note: Corbet includes *Dinaromys bogdanovi, Microtus epiroticus, M. guentheri, M. cabrerae, Pitymys bavaricus, P. tatricus, P. liechtensteini*]

Family Cricetidae
Cricetus cricetus — Common hamster
[Note: Corbet includes *Mesocricetus newtoni and Cricetulus migratorius*]

Family Microtidae
Ondatra zibethicus — Muskrat

239

CHECKLIST OF SPECIES

Family Capromyidae
Myocastor coypus   Coypu

Family Castoridae
Castor fiber   European beaver
Castor canadensis   Canadian beaver

Family Spalacidae
Mircospalax leucodon   Lesser mole rat
Spalax polonicus   Podlie mole rat
Spalax micropthalmus   Greater mole rat

Family Hystricidae
Hystrix cristata   Porcupine

Order Lagomorpha

Family Leporidae
Lepus capensis   Brown hare
Lepus timidus   Variable hare
Oryctolagus cuniculus   Rabbit
Sylvilagus floridanus   Florida rabbit

Order Artiodactyla

Family Suidae
Sus scrofa   Wild boar

Family Cervidae
Cervus elaphus   Red deer
Cervus nippon   Sika deer
Dama dama   Fallow deer
Alces alces   Elk
Capreolus capreolus   Roe deer

[Note: Corbet includes *Cervus axis, Odocoileus virginianus, Muntiacus reevsi, hydropotes inermis*]

Family Bovidae
Ovis ammon   Mouflon
Capra ibex   Alpine ibex
Capra pyrenaica   Spanish ibex
Rupicapra rupicapra   Chamois
Rupicapra ornata   Isard

[Note: Corbet includes *Ovibos moschatus*]